Contemporary Sculpture and the Critique of Display Cultures

I0461802

In this book, Dan Adler addresses recent tendencies in contemporary art toward assemblage sculpture and how these works incorporate tainted materials – often things left on the side of the road, according to the logic and progress of the capitalist machine – and combine them in ways that allow each element to retain a degree of empirical specificity. Adler develops a range of aesthetic models through which these practices can be understood to function critically. Each chapter focuses on a single exhibition: Isa Genzken's "OIL" (German Pavilion, Venice Biennale, 2007), Geoffrey Farmer's midcareer survey (Musée d'art contemporain, Montréal, 2008), Rachel Harrison's "Consider the Lobster" (CCS Bard Hessel Museum of Art, 2009), and Liz Magor's "The Mouth and Other Storage Facilities" (Henry Art Gallery, Seattle, 2008).

Dan Adler is Associate Professor of Modern and Contemporary Art History at York University in Toronto.

Routledge Focus on Art History and Visual Studies

Advancing a Different Modernism
SA Mansbach

Contemporary Sculpture and the Critique of Display Cultures
Tainted Goods
Dan Adler

Contemporary Sculpture and the Critique of Display Cultures
Tainted Goods

Dan Adler

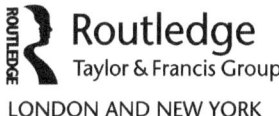
Routledge
Taylor & Francis Group

LONDON AND NEW YORK

First published 2019 by Routledge

2 Park Square, Milton Park, Abingdon, Oxfordshire OX14 4RN

52 Vanderbilt Avenue, New York, NY 10017

Routledge is an imprint of the Taylor & Francis Group, an informa business

First issued in paperback 2020

Library of Congress Cataloging-in-Publication Data
Names: Adler, Dan (Daniel Allan), author.
Title: Contemporary sculpture and the critique of display cultures : tainted goods / Daniel Adler.
Description: New York : Routledge, 2019. |
Series: [Routledge focus on art history and visual studies] |
Includes bibliographical references and index.
Identifiers: LCCN 2018025953 | ISBN 9781138479623 (hardback) |
ISBN 9781351049177 (adobe) | ISBN 9781351049160 (epub) |
ISBN 9781351049153 (mobi)
Subjects: LCSH: Assemblage (Art) | Refuse as art material.
Classification: LCC N6498.A8 A35 2018 | DDC 702.81/4–dc23
LC record available at https://lccn.loc.gov/2018025953

ISBN: 978-1-138-47962-3 (hbk)
ISBN: 978-0-367-51604-8 (pbk)

Typeset in Times New Roman
by Out of House Publishing

Contents

Illustrations

Acknowledgements

This book has been a long time in the making. The project began with a conference, appropriately titled "Tainted Goods," that I organized with Barbara Fischer at the Centre for German and European Studies, York University and the Justina M. Barnicke Gallery, University of Toronto, in May of 2012. The German Academic Exchange Service (DAAD) generously supported this project, and I am grateful to the participants: Diedrich Diederichsen, Markus Hallensleben, Richard Hill, Gabriele Knapstein, Elizabeth Legge, Melanie O'Brian, Susanne Pfeffer, and Juliane Rebentisch. The discussion and debate at this event motivated me to write this book, much of which was written as a Visiting Scholar at Massey College, University of Toronto (2012–13). Since then, I have presented portions of this project at various venues. A big thank you goes to Jeannette Redensek for her comments and criticisms—and for chairing a session with me on contemporary assemblage practices at the College Art Association Conference in New York; the work of one of the session's speakers, Isabelle Graw, has a special resonance for this book. Thanks to Georgina Jackson, former co-director of Mercer Union, Toronto, for the opportunity to give a speculative talk during an earlier stage of writing. More recently, I lectured about Liz Magor's assemblages at the Kunstverein in Hamburg; thanks to the Kunstverein's director, Bettina Steinbrügge, for the kind invitation. And for their generous and critical feedback, I am grateful to those participating in a graduate seminar on the history and theory of assemblage at my institution, York University, in which I presented in-progress material. And of course, many thanks go to Isabella Vitti, Editor at Routledge, for her expert advice and supportive comments, and to Joshua Tranen for kind and efficient editorial assistance. I am immensely grateful to each of the four artists whose exhibitions I address in this volume: Geoffrey Farmer, Isa Genzken, Rachel Harrison, and Liz Magor. For many years, I have found their practices to be rewarding and enriching. With image permissions, I very much appreciate the help of Katharina Forero de Mund at Gallery Buchholz, Cologne; Tim Gentles and

Eleonore Hugendubel at Greene Naftali Gallery, New York; and Steven Cottingham at Catriona Jeffries Gallery, Vancouver. For her unflagging support and faith in me, and for her nudging to get it done, I am forever indebted to my partner, Kristin Campbell. This book is dedicated to our son, Jacob.

Introduction

This book is, in the main, about sculpture. It deals with artworks that feature sprawling accumulations of objects: some found, some modified, some handcrafted. I explore how these works employ the method of assemblage, incorporating tainted materials—often things literally left on the side of the road according to the logic and progress of the capitalist machine—and combining them in ways that allow each element to retain a degree of empirical specificity.[1] The materials tend to be fragmentary, and are juxtaposed with other items that initially may seem incompatible, so that in the end, they "say" nothing with communicative clarity. The book is an account of my own speculative experiences while confronting such indirect and disjunctive qualities, charting a course through the spaces of an exhibition. My frequent focus on how these shows critique various "display cultures" might seem to reduce such artworks merely to instruments of materialist critique. I seek, however, to develop a broader range of aesthetic models through which these sculptural practices can be understood to function critically, whether as commentaries on capitalist economies, as anthropologies of everyday life, as critiques of the practices of museum collecting and interpretation, as twisted replications of sales strategies from advertising, stores, and television shopping networks, or as surrenders to the psychologies of accumulation, be they sumptuous pleasure, emotional displacement, or pathologized hoarding behavior. The development of these models began with the study of a single, sprawling work in my book *Hanne Darboven: Cultural History, 1880–1983* (2009). The shows examined in *Tainted Goods* build upon this study, in that they all perform their critique of display cultures through the stark juxtaposition of materials that have not been permitted to blend seamlessly into a coherent compositional whole that may be consumed or marketed with ease.

The introductory sections of this book theorize, survey, and critique some recent and historical sculptural practices, stretching and playing with the notions of installation art, sculpture, and assemblage. This is followed by chapters that each focus in detail on a single exhibition:

Isa Genzken's "OIL" (German Pavilion, Venice Biennale, 2007), Geoffrey Farmer's midcareer survey (Musée d'art contemporain, Montreal, 2008), Rachel Harrison's "Consider the Lobster" (CCS Bard Hessel Museum of Art, 2009), and Liz Magor's "The Mouth and Other Storage Facilities" (Henry Art Gallery, Seattle, 2008). Despite the spatial expansiveness of these shows, I wish to stick to the concept of sculpture as a means to help distinguish my aesthetic position from others associated with an amorphous category: "installation art" in recent years has come to connote a context that is dictated increasingly by demands for the dazzle of eye candy, playground atmospheres, immersive spaces for lounging, and monumentality for its own sake—all designed to instill stimulating states of perceptual novelty, amused passivity, or technological awe.[2] It has been more than thirty years since Rosalind Krauss's essay "Sculpture in the Expanded Field" appeared. This account dealt with artworks that are neither painting nor sculpture, that opened themselves up to other categories, including architecture and landscape.[3] As Hal Foster has discussed, during these three decades, the expanded field has gradually imploded: terms once held in positive contradiction have collapsed into compounds without tension—as in the myriad combinations of pictorial and sculptural, or art and architecture, that thrive as so-called installation art today.[4] As Claire Bishop has explored, efforts to "activate" audiences are part of a prevailing trend of "relational" and participatory installation art—often portrayed in opposition to a mythic counterpart: passive spectatorial consumption. Since the 1990s, this trend has been fueled in part by an ethos of emancipation "from a state of alienation induced by the dominant ideological order—be this consumer capitalism, totalitarian socialism, or military dictatorship."[5] So-called participatory art "aims to restore and realize a communal, collective space of shared social engagement." But the spaces and behaviors generated by "relational" installations reflect a shift away from an audience which "enjoys its subordination to strange experiences devised for them by an artist, to an audience that is encouraged to be a co-producer of the work (and who, occasionally, can even get paid for this involvement)."[6] Before describing the set of aesthetic qualities which runs through the book, I will further consider the distinction between "participatory" installation and sculpture.

Rather than surveying the field of installation art, I will focus in detail on two examples by two artists: Carsten Höller and Rachel Whiteread. I selected their works—both produced for the Turbine Hall at Tate Modern—because they were seen by a great many people, and because of my own ambivalent attitudes to their respective projects (which I have often admired). It is because of this ambivalence that I attempt to do justice to the material and experiential qualities of their works—contending with the pleasures and promises that these installations offered to me—before reflecting on how and why they are, in important ways, symptomatic of larger tendencies in contemporary art. These tendencies include legions of relational and participatory works that are far less interesting and engaging.

The Promise and Presentness of Pleasure

Indeed, viewing Carsten Höller's exhibition *Test Site* (2006), held at Tate Modern, was a key moment when conceptualizing this project. For me, this show was an ideal opportunity to reflect on market-oriented pressures to expand museum displays in order to generate accumulated spectacles of a size that dramatically exceeds human scale, to the extent that critical awareness is diminished.[7] My argument is meant to respond to "brands" of massive installations that are designed and staged according to the principle of efficient delivery of pleasure and awe; these are often made up of objects that are stylistically similar—rather than juxtaposed disjunctively and drawn from ostensibly divergent contexts, as in the case of the assemblage-based works—forming spectacular displays that are perceptually unusual in ways which are carefully calculated to supply an edgy thrill or a seemingly subversive shiver.

Entering the Turbine Hall gallery, I confronted five enormous slides of differing lengths—52 to 190 feet in length—emanating from the fifth, fourth, third, and second floors of the building. Each one wrapped around a central pillar, and served to supply an expected thrill: a surging and spiral movement, more reminiscent of waterpark settings than playgrounds. The tallest and largest provided the most dramatic effect, as it projected sideways before descending into a steep and accelerating curve. After a few tries, I noticed some design qualities: the slides' clear plastic ceilings, the ribs placed at regular intervals, allowing for blurred succession of accelerating lines while in transit. But the buzz, of course, came from a sense of disorientation, fueled in part by mild unease about the product's structural integrity, akin to that felt on a rollercoaster. By taking a turn, one chooses to give up control, surrendering to an experience that incorporates fear bathed in nostalgia, harkening back to childhood playgrounds, as sites of repetitive play, performing the same gesture, with slight variation, as a means of letting off steam.[8] I later lounged on the floor momentarily, noticing a skylight extending the length of the hall, shining upon the slides' stainless steel exteriors, glistening and glowing in ways evoking futuristic and utopian architectures. Some of the slides had terminuses in the same ground-floor area, where visitors congregated, allowing for a performance-based high—a feeling of being watched by others, either known or unknown, an awareness which is crucial, I will argue, to the design and appeal of such spectacular installations. As scores of online photographs attest (on social media sites), few gallery visitors actually contemplated *Test Site* as a sculptural phenomenon. It was primarily enjoyed in use, as it were, or as a novel form of communal space suitable for lounging, for chatting while waiting in line, or as a big, shiny, and unusual photographic backdrop. As with several other Turbine Hall exhibitions, Höller's show—with its theme-park scale and design—did not encourage productive or critical reflection on the conditions of its display, but rather helped to affirm those conditions. Jessica Morgan, the show's curator, emphasized that the slides reflected a concern with social change: they were "conceived not only as a pleasure-inducing ride" but served as a "grand advertisement, propaganda even, for the use of slides in our everyday landscape and architecture." Indeed, the slides were meant by Höller to test a hypothesis: that they supplied an effect of vertigo-induced exhilaration, joy, and lack of control—which could have a transformative effect on our behavior.[9] Dorothea von Hantelmann admires the way that visitors' experiences of Höller's slides were "not just an important part of the artwork; it *is* the work. The object becomes a device to transform us, to make us feel and exist differently. This cannot be right or wrong; it can only succeed or fail."[10]

For most visitors, *Test Site* provided a fun experience, which I define as a state of enjoyment that is immediately felt, with little or no complication. As Erica Weitzman has discussed, Adorno and Horkheimer's position against the immediate enjoyment of artworks was fairly clear, as they equated fun with notions of false consciousness and political idiocy. Fun is a term used to describe the most mind-numbing of the culture industry's products:

> The culture industry cheats its consumers of what it perpetually promises. The promissory note ... with its plots and staging, which draws on pleasure, it is endlessly prolonged; the promise, which is all the spectacle consists of, is illusory; all it actually confirms is that the real point will never be reached, that the diner must be satisfied with the menu.[11]

Adorno was particularly fascinated by an American context of pseudo-solidarity, in which people are conditioned to participate in amusements that are defined as "having fun," a performance of pleasurability that only serves to reinforce the status quo. Fun is the fake pleasure taken in normativity (e.g., weekend leisure activities that are dictated by labor schedules), in which we strive to display ourselves properly as socially functional citizens. Adorno describes the culture industry's infinite deferral of pleasure; it aims to reassure, to soothe, to distract, and to provide an escape valve for personal and sociological tensions of all kinds. He dismisses the argument that the system is satisfying real desires, giving customers what they want. The artwork must be "dissonant" in its refusal of the immediacy or presentness of pleasure. He argues that art must engage with this escape valve, as a counter-image intended in part to expose the tension between semblance and reality that the culture industry strives to suppress.[12]

Hal Foster has discussed the increasing prevalence of identity branding and design within a post-Fordist environment of tweaked commodities and niched markets.[13] In his polemical study, Foster asks several key questions, such as:

> To what extent has the 'constructed subject' of postmodernism become the 'designed subject' of consumerism, a perfect hybrid of marketing and culture, or something to be that is also something to buy? To what extent has the expanded field of postwar art become the administered space of contemporary design?

A crucial shift occurred during the 1980s, when corporate merging and cultural marketing expanded exponentially, so that everything— consumer objects and art—seemed to be regarded as so much *design*.[14] During this period, special seductions were devised, so that packaging became increasingly important compared with actual consumer goods. A product may be produced on a massive scale yet appear up-to-date, personal, and precise in address, so that we may react with the thought "hey, that's *me*."

Such a product may be a custom-made slide, or perhaps a high-end storage container, staged and showcased at an impressive venue like Tate Modern, in which visitors may sense an industrial gravitas, the accumulated weight of proletarian labor, exerted for so many decades on this riverbank site. Like Höller's *Test Site*, Rachel Whiteread's Turbine Hall exhibition *Embankment* (2005) was a gigantic installation, made up of industrially fabricated elements based, like the slides, on the same design concept and parameters. All interpretive and promotional material for Whiteread's show referred, like a mantra, to a central theme: the artist's discovery of an aged box in her mother's home shortly after she passed away. For the artist, this was obviously an object with a deeply metaphorical resonance. Initially, Whiteread decided to work with a cast of the interior of the box, with its frayed edges, tape residues, and various bumps and indentations. She then decided to make casts from a range of differently shaped boxes, to offer some product variation, as it were—filling them with plaster, peeling away the exteriors, so that the "ghostly" remains recorded and preserved all of the minute imperfections. However, she made a crucial change, re-designing the casts in a translucent white polyethylene, and then placing an order for 14,000, so as to situate them as a monumental display.

Entering the gallery, I immediately looked upwards, to the top of a stepped structure, a partial pyramid. Strolling about, I encountered groups of pillar- and wall-like arrangements, along with other rectilinear forms, placed in orderly rows. I proceeded down narrower alleyways, pausing to consider some formations that seemed relatively organic in design, and hence contrasting with the more architectural elements. However, the sheer accumulated enormity of Whiteread's installation— with its thousands of like monochrome units—discouraged intimate, detailed, or prolonged contemplation of any of its parts, or even an awareness that the boxes differed from each other. There was in the end, for me, only a general sense of the cubes as a slick, synthetic expression of a larger design concept. In smaller numbers, perhaps they would seem akin to customized storage systems for the home or office. Whiteread was supposedly inspired—along with the maternal memory mentioned earlier—by the storage warehouse depicted in the final scene of Steven Spielberg's *Raiders of the Lost Ark* (1981), in which the Ark of the Covenant is stored away (with other unseen treasures), among scores of wooden crates, each with its own processing number. Along with this cinematic reference, the Tate's website mentions Whiteread's critique of American Minimalism, in particular its penchant for pristine and indus- trially fabricated cubes, used by Donald Judd and his colleagues "to explore issues of repetition, the impersonality of mass production, and the relationship of the viewer's body to the space occupied by objects." Whiteread is said to respond to that tradition by making cubes which

> maintain the imprints of human use; they are stacked up in both ordered and disordered piles; and whilst they encourage us to think about the space they inhabit, en masse they are also a spec- tacle, an unforgettable image that reveals itself slowly as the viewer approaches … At one stage, Whiteread had considered making a single vast monumental sculpture for the Turbine Hall. Ironically, what she finally came up with is an anti-monument, a form collapsed back into a landscape.[15]

Observing viewers funneling through the installation, I could not help but disagree with these online words: Whiteread's was a show of monumental proportions. Any "imprints of human use" were suppressed by overall impressions of a seamless display featuring pris- tinely white plastic cubes, mass-produced and industrially-fabricated on a grand scale. Visitors' actual encounters in the gallery amounted, for the most part, to a mobile and mildly theatrical experience. As with Höller's *Test Site*, the work served as a novel environment—and an intriguing backdrop for chatting leisurely, hanging out with friends, or taking snapshots—a participatory and pleasant people-watching environment that was perceptually unusual and yet unchallenging. Indeed, it is viewers' awareness of somehow being observed by others—either in the here and now of gallery, or for a subsequent audience online, through photographic documents—within such a dramatic space, and surrounded by a specially designed white and hygienic architecture—a brand-new monumental structure, untainted by use, with a contrasting old shell, sandblasted and gutted so that presently it supplies a tasteful industrial patina. Indeed, Whiteread supplied a fashionable stage for me to "perform" for others: crucially, this audience, literal or imagined, may consist of specific individuals (a partner, a friend), a peer group (that may see my snapshots online), or an institution, any one of which I might wish to please, by demonstrating—either in the institution or "live" on Twitter—that I am getting some culture and having a good time doing it. When telling my tale of visiting Tate Modern, perhaps with my smart phone as a guide—diligently shooting the scene for YouTube—I can speak about Whiteread's striking and smart-looking project, pointing to the pleasingly "minimal" white products surrounding me and, with calm confidence, mention a pair of reference points—a movie and a maternal memory—that provided interpretive keys, allowing me to "get" the work and retain a singular, lasting memory of the exhibition experience.

One of the most influential guides for marketing strategists, B. Joseph Pine II and James H. Gilmore's *The Experience Economy: Work is Theatre and Every Business a Stage* (1999) compares theatrical productions with "active" experiences in retail, theme-park, hotel, and museum settings.[16] Guests in these venues should feel as though they are on stage, sensing that someone else is watching; this feeling of playing a role may help enormously to distinguish a memorable experience from an ordinary one:[17] "That's why we call such buyers *aspirants*, who wish to be someone or something different. Without change in attitude, performance, characteristics, or some other dimension of the self, no such transformation occurs." The transformative aspect seems to affect "the very being of the buyer" because it seems tailored and individual. Accordingly, it is crucial to stage scenarios that are not overly optimistic (or challenging) in their goals.[18] Pine and Gilmore emphasize certain innovations during the 1980s when Ian Schrager, for instance, turned hotel lobbies into "unique experiences," staging them as distinctive, hip lounge areas. These experiences were designed around a central theme with "positive cues" contributing to its impression as a "mnemonic place," a tool that aids in the creation of singular, lasting memories. To help ensure guest engagement, theming requires scripting a storyline—as in the case of "socially progressive" slides or the notion of a museum as a "warehouse" of memories—and a coordinated series of signals: perceptual phenomena generated by landscaping, graphics, scents, recorded music, handrail surfaces, and so on.[19]

For Pine and Gilmore, "mass customization" describes the production of standardized modules, combined in different ways for different buyers, as in the case of personal technologies (phones, tablets, etc.) with the built-in potential for alteration according to individual taste and needs, so that the product or service is staged in the venue so that it seems unique and precious—and delivers what subjects think they want. The customized retail experience, accordingly, offers to fulfill a promise by appearing to alter a product—in terms of features, as well as its description, framing, packaging, placement, name, or stated use. In addition, Pine and Gilmore stress how helpful it is to achieve some sort of customer surprise, by staging something perceptually unexpected, although never truly disjunctive, disturbing, or disorienting. These experiential goals are reached by calculating variables related to value (collaborative and mutually determined, or cosmetic and visually demonstrated), process (sharable or adjustable), nature of interaction (direct, indirect, overt, covert), method of learning (conversation, solicitation, recognition, observation), and basis of the experience (exploring, experimenting, gratifying, discovering).[20] And customer experiences may be orchestrated according to a theatrically derived narrative, in which an aspirant literally plays a role in discovering something about him- or herself, by enacting gestures or prescribed experiments in a venue: exposition (introduction to the context), inciting incident (setting the action in motion), rising action (rapidly increasing possibilities and intensity), crisis (heightened activities and obstacles), climax (of the many things that could happen, only one does), falling action (resulting consequences), and dénouement (tying together plot threads, and a return to normalcy).

It is telling that Höller's first large-scale show in the US was called "Experience" (New Museum, New York, 2011) and was filled with a range of performative and participatory works that are reminiscent of the range of variables and goals discussed in Pine and Gilmore's book. *Giant Psycho Tank* (1999), for instance, allowed for a literally immersive experience akin to a spa treatment, punctuated by an exhibitionist thrill of performing—with the "customized" feature of either donning swim trunks or taking the plunge *au naturel*—as a passive, sensorially deprived subject, hence playing a role for an (unseen) museum public, for the scientist's cold medical gaze, or for those waiting in the (theatrical) wings. Guests (or customers) could bathe individually in a translucent white polypropylene container—strangely akin to Whiteread's boxes—installed, appropriately, on a stage, filled with Epsom-salted water heated to 98 degrees Fahrenheit. *The Pinocchio Effect* (1999) was similarly based on a novel "experimental" premise, designed for a pair of subjects, instructed to apply vibrating medical devices while holding their noses. Other installations, such as *The Forest* (2002), *Upside-Down Goggles* (2009/2011), and *Infrared Room* (2004), were typical in that they required a form of temporary bodily investment or compliance, by putting on devices such as 3D goggles or infrared cameras, in the presence of spectators or others waiting their turn. Quite reliably, each work was designed to supply a carefully calibrated thrill: as a form of altered perception, seemingly geared for each user, that includes novel screen-based imagery which represents performers' bodies, documenting and verifying that they were there, that they subjected themselves to these technologies within a setting fashioned according to two "theming" narratives: the playground and the laboratory. The exhibition's catalogue supports such claims, with the curator, Massimiliano Gioni, stating that Höller's art "engages our senses in a way that is once entertaining and critical, spectacular and subtle, providing immersive work that is "part amusement park, part laboratory."[21] Elsewhere, Nicolas Bourriaud argues for the criticality of Höller's works, which function as "devices designed to make us question our relationship with the world and our perceptions of physical reality." Bourriaud emphasizes and lauds the impressive range of effects available to museum visitors: "Hypnotic and cathartic states, hallucinations, hilarity, suspension of judgment, intoxication, profound doubt—the list of mental states, moral reactions, and physical sensations generated by Höller's work would seem one of the most complete ever produced by a single artist."[22] I would argue that, for the most part, Höller's show did not provoke profound doubt but rather forms of altered perception akin to entertainments in a high-end amusement park or a cutting-edge science center.[23]

Subverting the Seamless and Setting the Stage

Indeed, Höller's New Museum show is symptomatic of a wider trend—among galleries, museums, fairs, and biennials—to supply experiences that are fun, and often monumental in scale, in uncomplicated ways. It is crucial to speak here of staged viewing experiences that run along a circuit of design, production, and consumption activities which are connected seamlessly: themed display strategies and participatory qualities help to ensure that this circuit runs with optimal efficiency. In this book, I interpret some assemblage-based sculptural practices that *ride this circuit while also subverting it*, by provoking viewing experiences that are neither seamless nor easily consumed. In the remainder of this introduction, I would like to explore a set of structural features which—when effectively combined—encourage experiences that are fun and not-fun, inviting and challenging, seductive and complicated.[24] My main purpose in this book is to focus on these structural qualities rather than on "contextual" material—as it is conventionally conceived by art writers, and associated with the monographic study of each of the artists addressed. For example, I will not be dealing in detail or directly with the important roles that the artists' formative periods—for example, in Berlin, New York, or Vancouver—may play in the making of meaning in their works. Rather, I emphasize certain qualities that their artworks share, traits which ensure that the circuit of semantic communication becomes disrupted and less immediate—short-circuiting, as it were, habitual cultures of efficient transmission from speaker to hearer, from marketer to consumer.

In the post-structuralist tradition, I subscribe to the strategy of critiquing and questioning—while never dismissing or wholly erasing—mythologies of the authorial ego, exposing them, as Roland Barthes put it, to the cacophony of contradictory thoughts that are possible when encountering any text. This questioning is well suited to the effects of dissolution and disjunction felt—between subject and object, between found and handmade, between literal and abstract imagery, and so on—during encounters with the assemblage-based displays featured in this book. My main concern is with the synchronic investigation of a specific set of practices during the recent past (as when the structuralist freezes a certain language at given moment to better comprehend its functioning principles), rather than with the diachronic study of a sculptural genre evolving over time (as when one studies etymological or phonetic change in a language over decades of development). The four main shows that I address actually all took place roughly a decade ago. However, the reader will see that this book is obviously not a strict adherent to structuralism: the focus is not upon abstract systems of rules at the expense of concrete, individual happenings produced within those systems: my interest is not solely in language rather than speech, in linguistic competence rather than performance, in structure rather than event.[25] Rather, I provide a narrative that documents my own experiences as a performer moving through the gallery space: each chapter provides a play-by-play account of one encounter with an exhibition, a subjective struggle to come to terms with a series of staged scenarios. Considered together, these narratives collectively serve as "spoken" case studies, as incarnations of a sculptural structure called "tainted goods."

In crafting these narratives, I am indebted to Georges Didi-Huberman's discussions of speculative art history, particularly when confronting works featuring disjunctive elements that are resistant to states of seamless synthesis. When faced with such a display, the beholder (or writer) may choose to know without seeing or to see without knowing.

He who chooses only *to know* will have gained, of course, the unity of synthesis and the self-evidence of simple reason; but he will lose the real of the object, in the symbolic closure of the discourse that reinvents the object in its own image, or rather in its own representation.[26]

Those who desire to see are prepared to lose the unity of the enclosed world, running the risk of death for the subject of knowledge, or the risk of not-knowledge when synthesis becomes fragile to the point of collapse. I wish to respond to the need to return to a questioning of the image that does not yet presuppose the "figured figure"—which is fixed as a representational object—but contends with the "figuring figure," which may be defined as a process by which we remain in a constraining (but endlessly productive) dilemma, shifting between states of knowing and seeing. Didi-Huberman elaborates this process as one of active figuration that—little by little or all of a sudden—makes multiple elements touch that previously were separated: they bang together in a chaos (*Mischbildung*) that may render impossible their efficient recognition as terms, so that the process of intelligible subsumption breaks down. Under these disjunctive conditions, the presented terms may undergo a process of *de-meaning*, a term that for me carries a great deal of interpretive weight, as I associate the tainted goods aesthetic with an unexpected condition of empathy (and sometimes sympathy) sparked by encounters with a series of subjects that have been reduced to objects (and vice versa). In contrast to the packaged *installation* experiences critiqued earlier, this book focuses on subjective encounters with *exhibitions* populated predominantly by sculptural forms that may also be figures—along with other kinds of objects that compete with the idea of the coherent figure.

Tainted goods are de-meaned partially because they are assemblages that make reference to combinations of contexts in abrupt and unresolved ways: occupying a human scale and exhibiting signs of figuration, they aspire to be fully fledged characters—centered in their presentation of easily identifiable identities—but they fail to do so, coming across as flawed, faulty, and fragmented. They perform badly as characters partly because their bodies incorporate found things and reductive, abstract shapes which have been handcrafted. And they are often made up of humble, non-precious, and oddly outdated stuff, allowing them to appear as entities that have been forced—often absurdly, often pathetically—into a predicament, as material that is struggling to matter, to be something (and/or someone) worthy of attention, despite their difference from conventionally coherent characters with more obvious currency as products.[27] These anti-characters seem tainted, offering few coherent qualities. And yet they are still worth the struggle to know, a struggle that is ongoing and often precarious.

Crafting Crappy Characters: Humorously Holding on to the Human

Like Pine and Gilmore, my interpretive approach is set within the context of the stage, one that is informed by the theatre of the absurd, by philosophies that foreground notions of the performing spectator, and by discourses that address the "theatricality" and latent anthropomorphism of minimalist art. Samuel Beckett's *Play* (1962) offers characters that fall prey to reductivism and repetitiveness, both in terms of visual appearance and dialogue: three heads appear on stage, protruding from urns, framed against darkness. They are situated so that spectators feel that they share the space of performance with those onstage. Their faces appear almost as inanimate as the urns; only their mouths and eyes move. A spotlight moves rapidly from one head to another, provoking them into speaking, or plunges them into silence and darkness, creating a verbal and visual rhythm that partly replaces dialogue and scenic action. These "performers" do seem under duress and not quite present as characters (or actors) in the conventional sense—existing in limbo between subject and object, between present and past, offering no stable sense of self, encouraging the audience to try (and fail) to ascribe to them further qualities, as embodied personas, figured figures that could then be recognized coherently, that are indisputably there in the present, as commodities with currency.[28] Rather, spectators shift between different spectatorial conditions: witnessing, judging, sympathizing, collaborating, or interrogating. As subjects and objects, these bodies, as Anna McMullan puts it, are "curiously provisional," to the extent that we seem to be bearing "witness to the traces of a human existence on the verge of extinction."[29] Indeed, their currency as characters seems to be fading before our eyes, caught up irrevocably in the process of obsolescence.

As Agnes Heller has discussed, existential comedies—in which the characters do not play historically or socially known roles, and yet antagonisms obviously exist between them—are stylized in ways that do not register as "generalization or idealization, but the presentation of significant marginality as the carrier of the human condition ..." Characters must be seen as playing roles that are unsuited to them; they are subject to spells of repetitive and dysfunctional behavior, intended to poke fun at idealistic beliefs, the desire for redemption, or sentimentality. But while paradoxes are dissolved with conventional jokes, they remain unresolved in existential comedies: "Whatever is ridiculed is also mourned; the thing that has been lost is mocked, but the loss still hurts. An aura of mysticism can surround the absurd drama."[30] In Beckett's *Waiting for Godot*, the character Vladimir opens the second act by singing an old song about a dog stealing a bone from a kitchen and is beaten to death by the cook; the song is repeated *ad nauseum*. For Heller, more immediate comedy has contradictions that seem relatively painless for the audience, while existential comedy is less obvious, and more prone to subjective projection of meanings, depending on spectators' respective abilities to reflect and on how they each perceive (or detect) irony and other forms of humor.[31]

My encounters with exhibitions in this book are inspired by Beckett's stage productions. I wish to read shows according to a conception of the theatre which encompasses spectators, performing with other (non)actors and entities within an exhibition space. Jacques Rancière theorizes theatre within a broad field of visual culture, potentially within any experience that "place[s] bodies in action before an assembled audience."[32] He argues for the need to blur the boundaries between those who act and those who look; between individuals and members of a collective body. I would argue that it is the consistent incorporation of found, everyday objects into a human-scaled topography of tainted goods—a stage where spectators may become performers in ways that avoid the unchallenging and packaged "experiences" that I have previously discussed. Indeed, Rancière critiques recent art forms of "consumerist hyper-activism," pointing out a pervasive tendency to create hybridized experiences composed of means to facilitate a dazzling, novel, and constant exchange of roles and identities—the real and the virtual, the organic and the mechanical—as in the case of "experimental" scenarios with slick AV displays.[33] For Rancière, these forms of spectacle lead to a condition of "stultification, which uses the blurring of boundaries and the confusion of roles to enhance the effect of the performance without questioning its principles." Instead of amplifying and diversifying perceptual effects on the monumental scale of a theme park, Rancière argues for the need for spectatorial encounters with phenomena that problematize the cause–effect relationship itself and that question the set of presuppositions which sustain the logic of stultification. I wish to encourage the practice of narrating and translating the conglomerations of characters and things being staged in the gallery, as I strive to do in each chapter of this book.

Rancière emphasizes the fictional component of this narration and translation, citing how—through subtraction and addition—the aesthetic work transforms given bodies into new ones: the mutilated Hercules becomes the Deleuzian "body without organs"; Vico reinvents a new figure of the "poet" loosely deriving from Homer's poetry; Winckelmann makes a model of ideal sculpture by verbally reinventing the shape of a few Greek statues. But every spectator-performer may strive to construct characters that reflect a release of potentialities—of new, as yet unseen, bodies.[34] However, Rancière reminds us that this "... effect occurs under the condition of an original disjunction ... which is the suspension of any direct relationship between cause and effect. The aesthetic effect is initially an effect of dis-identification. The aesthetic community is a community of dis-identified persons." We should strive to encounter an exhibition as a stage in which processes of dissociation may be enacted, causing breaks in relationships between what is seen and what is thought, or between what is thought and what is felt. Such breaks can happen anywhere and at any time.[35]

Another feature central to my thinking about tainted goods is the incorporation of minimal, reductive, and often geometric forms within an assemblage work that, despite the abstraction, aspires to be figural in some way and is resolute in its maintenance of a human scale.[36] This quality may be associated with discourse generated by Michael Fried's reaction to the theatrical experience of glimpsing minimalist sculpture: as Fried once stated:

> In fact, being distanced by such objects is not, I suggest, entirely unlike being distanced, or crowded, by the silent presence of another person; the experience of coming upon literalist objects unexpectedly—for example, in somewhat darkened rooms—can be strongly, if momentarily, disquieting in just this way.[37]

Juliane Rebentisch has recently reflected on how, despite its radical simplicity, minimal art takes on quasi-subjective qualities without wearing them on their sleeve; these artworks are theatrical in their double presence as things and as signs (*als Ding und als Zeichen*). For Rebentisch the oscillation between thing and sign can never be fully or neatly resolved into packaged meanings. Drawing upon ground-breaking discussions by Georges Didi-Huberman, Rebentisch reads minimalism as structurally uncanny: its material qualities come across as productive of meaning, but they are "merely" a speculative projection of meaning: nothing really legitimates these anthropomorphic speculations, and so they remain tentative and abstract, so that the "viewer is referred back to the facticity of the material whose supposed evidentness now also proves to be unstable—it is contaminated by latent meanings."[38] These tainted meanings, as I call them, are neither object-ively legible in the work nor "made" by the viewer. The material and abstract qualities of the object address the viewer as one who contributes to the production of meaning, but who is denied a sense of seamless resolution. At the very moment that the minimalist object seems to have taken on an anthropomorphic significance in the eyes of the viewer, a crisis of confidence may occur, as it is equally clear that nothing about this significance can be objectively proven: the production of meaning proves to be a projection of meaning. I should confront the object as a performative agent without exercising complete control over such forces which "befall" me. Rebentisch rightly argues that such art should not be read as disavowing itself by functioning as mere means for the transmission of prepackaged social or political issues. Quality works resist being reduced to the sociological investigations of museum audiences because their meanings are constitutively open: the political dimension unfolds within an aesthetic mode. Art does not become socially relevant by conveying particular content that could be communicated with better success and precision by omitting "art-like" decoration— as though form were merely an external addition to that content. But "form constitutes itself as aesthetic only insofar as it reflects the process of aesthetic experience playing back and forth between material and meaning."[39]

Predicaments: Crucial Combinations of Contexts and a Selected Set of Sculptural Sources

There are several additional qualities which run through the structure of sculpture called *tainted goods*. These qualities all relate to the staging of disjunctive combinations: multiple display contexts are referred to simultaneously (retail, museum, domestic, among others); abstract and literal elements are brought together abruptly; found objects are juxtaposed with materials that appear handmade; and newer elements are interspersed with products and images which seem outdated, or on the verge of obsolescence.[40] Encountering these combinatory qualities within a series of human-scaled assemblages that do seem somehow to be aspiring to be figures—despite their disjunctive contents, their partial abstraction, and their dysfunctional ability to offer coherent identities—there is a tendency toward empathetic (or even sympathetic) reactions. These figures seem caught up, or struggling, within a predicament, within a world that wants only centered and packaged selves that may easily and efficiently be consumed.

Throughout this book, I interpret this predicament in a host of ways, sometimes identifying it as a symptom of specific problems, or with a broader conception of the culture industry, but there is always an association with the disabling and dehumanizing costs of capitalist ideologies—forces that have profound effects upon our abilities to think and feel in the material realm, of things and people.[41] For me, the predicament is best expressed sculpturally, with mostly material means. It is crucial to show how matter can still matter as part of an effort to be critically aware, of the potential to throw a wrench into workings of the consumerist machine. To be in a predicament is to be caught up in a difficult, perplexing, or trying situation—a bind, a box, a corner, a hole, an impasse, a jam, a mire, a pickle, a rabbit hole, a rattrap, a sticky wicket, a kettle of fish. This little list of synonyms and definitions (derived from Merriam-Webster) seems analogous to assemblage, including its association with absurdity and a range of tangible and bodily implications, particularly those associated with fragmentation and abuse. With tainted goods, the beholder must contend with a concept of self that is straining to reach a state of comfortable coherence. The predicament is integral to an identity formed in uneasy dialogue with several display cultures simultaneously, a dialogue that therefore resists motives of efficient marketing, packaging, and sale.[42]

The *tainted goods* structure has complex roots and historical reference points that include Dada, Cubist, Surrealist, and Neo-Dada assemblage, along with many contemporary tendencies. Others have already astutely addressed some of these tendencies, often in monographic contexts—for instance, in the case of Harrison's complex relationships to the Duchampian readymade, to Robert Rauschenberg's Combines, and to crucial, recent figures such as Cady Noland and Franz West.[43] These roots include a number of highly influential exhibitions. One recent and prominent example was the ambitious "Unmonumental" show (New Museum, New York, 2007–8), which surveyed a diverse range of practices—including those by Genzken and Harrison—that juxtapose humble materials and fragmented forms in ways that critique cultures of spectacle and monumentality. In the exhibition catalogue, Massimiliano Gioni similarly distinguishes between *unmonumental* tendencies and installation-art experiences

> imbued with the same grandiosity associated with monumental sculpture. It is not accidental that the triumph of installation art has run parallel to that of an economy of spectacles and short attention spans. Installation art reflects the bombardment of data that shapes the mature phase of the information society. It describes the ecstasy of communication, the sublime realization of being just a knot in an ever-expanding flux of instant connections across the globe.[44]

And Trevor Smith refers to the provisional and structurally precarious nature of sculptures that are human-scaled, made from non-precious stuff—and yet appear as if they are formed by one person. Crucially, Smith addresses how these works do not define or transform an environment, but rather occupy a "contained sculptural space that draws attention through and across material surfaces whose portents remain unclear, oblique and defiantly minor key." Indeed, my approach to staging in *Tainted Goods* reflects the unmonumental's *descent* from a memorial space of the monument to a materialist world of "behavioral space" while also an *ascent* into an idealist world that lies beyond any specific site.[45] Other recent shows and publications have featured survey accounts of this and related tendencies, touching upon several ideological and aesthetic issues which are central to my account.[46] However, in *Tainted Goods* I wish to provide a more sustained reading, one that probes its formal, disjunctive, semantic, and critical aspects in greater detail—and within the focused, performative contexts of moving through individual exhibitions.

One historical, and truly pivotal, exhibition was William C. Seitz's "The Art of Assemblage," held in 1961 at the Museum of Modern Art in New York.[47] As with "Unmonumental," Seitz's vast show may be read as a display that upheld, extended, exceeded, and antagonized previous notions of what an assemblage (or a sculpture) can or should be. This event pronounced a definition of assemblage—of how and why we may juxtapose disparate elements in unexpected ways, releasing an unaccountable jolt of new meaning. Each element retains its separate identity and continues to tug in its own direction. An illuminating condition of "wrongness"—of different parts' irreconcilable "otherness"—results, along with a sense that the conflicting elements somehow attract each other even as they are repelled.[48] The opposed elements' uneasy proximity—the stress of their simultaneous attraction and repulsion—becomes the work's defining characteristic. This trait is associated with the metaphorical mistake, as when we present facts belonging to one class of objects in the idiom(s) belonging to another—literally "mistaking" one class for another.[49] Seitz's show at MoMA powerfully expressed a postwar "Neo-Dada" or "junk" aesthetic and its modernist heritage, surveying a remarkable diversity of practices ranging from cubism to the present.

The exhibition included two particularly provocative works by Ed Kienholz, *John Doe* (1959) and *Jane Doe* (1960), shown within an alcove space. Composed of the severed head and torso of a mannequin placed on a beat-up baby stroller, *John Doe* features a giant wooden arrow—sandwiched between stroller and corpus—that functions as a base for this divided man, who shows additional signs of abuse and neglect. A plaque, mounted on the front of the stroller, is reminiscent of a panhandler's sign. It reads: "Riddle: Why is John Doe like a piano? Answer: Because he is square, upright, and grand. – Old Soothe Saying." For *Jane Doe*, Kienholz attached a female child doll's head to a cabinet with drawers, and then covered the sculpture up to the neck with the skirt from an ornate bridal gown. When this soiled garment is lifted, one discovers drawers containing trinkets meant to symbolize her sexual and emotional secrets. Her true feelings remain concealed. She is portrayed as an object, a piece of furniture.

Kienholz's assemblages were intended in part as a satirical attack upon the idea of the heroic and vigorous male (and his subservient bride), which he associated with the dehumanizing effects of American consumerist, imperialist, and consumerist ideologies. Such heroes, mythologized in postwar film (John Wayne, Cary Grant), were rendered by Kienholz as disabled and demeaned, infantile and impotent. John Doe's penis is hidden away in a secret compartment in the back of the stroller. And his smile suggests the self-deceiving fiction of his emotional and religious beliefs. A radiating star at the center of his chest, once the symbol of heroic deeds and universal love, has opened to reveal a wooden cross instead of a heart. A metal stovepipe runs from the back of his torso directly to the cross, as if to suggest that this hollow man is only blowing hot air when devotion to God and his fellow citizens are concerned. The hole in the center oozes and drips bloody red paint.[50] However, given their disjunctive and fragmentary composition—of literal and abstract elements, of newer and obsolete commodities, of found and handmade elements, of textual and material representation, of references to multiple cultures of display simultaneously—Kienholz's works exceed any specific contexts of satire and therefore are particularly relevant to the tainted goods aesthetic. As Seitz states:

> As element is set beside element, the many qualities and auras of isolated fragments are compounded, fused or contradicted so that—by their own confronted volitions, as it were—physical matter becomes poetry ... a vast repertoire of expression—exultant, bitter, ironic, poetic, or lyrical—can be achieved by means different in kind from that of painting and sculpture ...[51]

Surrealist exhibition design was a crucial reference point for Kienholz, especially those shows featuring assemblage works combining fragmentary mannequins with a host of other materials. As with tainted goods, these shows emphasized the successive and staged encounter with multiple works which each aspire (and fail) to be fully fledged figures or coherent characters. This failure to cohere occurred within the context of an expansive, yet mostly human-scaled, exhibition. Among the most influential of these sprawling shows was the "Exposition international du surréalisme," held in Paris in 1938. It included 16 mannequins greeting visitors, each designed by a different artist, situated along a long narrow room along with fictional and found street signs. Many exhibited signs of abuse and humiliation: Andre Masson's, for example, had her head in a birdcage and her mouth gagged with a velvet band, while Jean Arp's was carefully decorated and covered with a plastic bag.[52] In addition, Duchamp fitted the ceiling with 1,200 sacks of "coal" hanging from the ceiling (they actually only contained paper), imparting a grotto-like effect that was vaguely threatening within the confined space, a feeling of unease enhanced by fine coal dust and crepuscular lighting designed by Man Ray.[53] Obviously engaging in a satirical dialogue with European retail culture, this display offered disjunctive diversities of readymade and handmade materials, conglomerations envisioned by some surrealists as resistant to stylistically unified artistic languages associated with singular forms and materials, and to more general notions of bourgeois good taste and (art) goods. Significantly, surrealists often applied the term "objet" rather than "sculpture" to help discourage associations with traditional aesthetics, identified with medium specificity and institutional compatibility. Crucial to their compositional cocktails was the juxtaposition of utterly banal things (forgettable, unwanted, obsolete objects), often acquired at flea markets—transformed with acts of "controlled chance" that rejected conventional notions of artistic skill (sculptural or otherwise) and expressive authenticity. However, while such procedures were identified with notions of the arbitrary, they also reflected a sincere belief in the power of such ordinary objects to expose and express unconscious desires. Breton and Dali were particularly devoted to developing the "secret potential" of everyday things, enabling a productive transformation to occur so that the work "is absolutely useless from a practical and rational point of view and is created wholly for the purpose of materializing in a fetishistic way ..."[54]

Influenced by Surrealist aesthetics and materialism, Walter Benjamin's study of the Parisian Arcades explored cultures of collecting and display that inform the present-day terms of tainted goods: only within a display context of juxtaposition can "objects get their due" because each item is displaced from its original function and recontextualized. Benjamin envisioned collectors as historiographers whose materials were not textual but tactile. Each item's fate in the collector's display was determined by its recognition as having questionable value and reinserted within a new economy of signification, in which its use-value is fully altered and is allowed to affect beholders in subjective ways. "The true method of making things present is to represent them in our space (not to represent ourselves in their space) ... We don't displace our being into theirs; they step into our life."[55]

Such theorizations of collecting and display were conceived in some sense as responses to the capitalist predicament. At the heart of the predicament is the near-impossibility of thinking historically and dialectically, due in part to the longstanding ideological equation of freedom and the ability to consume. The mass media are in the service of the illusion that the proliferation of commodities is tantamount to human liberation. As Susan Buck-Morss has discussed, Benjamin's dialectical composition

> refers to the use of contradictory images to identify what is his-
> torically new about the 'nature' of commodities. The principle of
> construction is one of montage, whereby the image's ideational
> elements remain unreconciled, rather than fusing into one 'har-
> monizing perspective'.

Benjamin strove to introduce the transitory into the seemingly eternal mythic form of the commodity as wish image.[56] In their origins, commodities were signifiers of the utopian, liberatory possibilities of human endeavor and industrialism. The process of commodification turns wish image into fetish, which is subject to decay. When the aura of goods disintegrates, this makes them ideal material for assembling a discontinuous construction, a staging of fragments from past and present. The objects are seized from disparate contexts—removed from the historicist's comfy historical continuum—and staged in order to conjure a revelatory "lightning flash" of insight about the present and future.

This beholding experience was identified with a straying from ideologies of compartmentalized knowledge, traditionally practiced by the museum. The straying or drifting activity—which is never an outright dismissal or abandonment—epistemologically informs the tainted goods aesthetic. William Seitz's MoMA exhibition included Joseph Cornell's pioneering assemblages, fashioned with an associative sensibility and incorporating prosaic and decaying bits of everyday objects. However, compared to tainted goods, Cornell's works are presented in a compartmentalized and contained manner as boxes and come across as relatively intimate and precious in significance—and often dreamily devoted to a dominant motif, such as a press photograph of a film star. For example, *Untitled (Penny Arcade Portrait of Lauren Bacall)* (1945–46) combines an aging arcade contraption with a close-up image of the actress. The work suggests a complex set of feelings—loss and longing, desire and fear—and the viewer may become absorbed when dropping a small red ball through a small door in the upper right corner of the work, allowing it to roll down glass ramps, and then moving past Bacall's face. Cornell's works often reflect a domestic and devotional activity of recapturing and intensifying the feeling of being in the cinema and collecting memorabilia in the service of a single revered person. As Benjamin H. D. Buchloh has observed, for Cornell the "collector," the container still functioned as a framing device associated with the spatial and psychological interiority of experience, derived partially from the cultic spaces of the shrine and the votive painting, and from private images of commemoration—leading up to the obsessive secrecy of the private object and the fetish.[57]

Rauschenberg's Combine works more explicitly explored the boundary between public and private, displaying decentralized combinations of domestic objects and urban detritus in ways that are more directly related to tainted goods. Faded fabrics, furniture fragments, worn-out domestic objects, scraps of newspaper, old snapshots—all in some sense evoking the contexts of both the street and the attic—conjure a temporal limbo between past and present, and posit a tension between use and obsolescence, meaning and irrelevance. For instance, in the MoMA show Seitz included Rauschenberg's *Canyon* (1959), a Combine featuring a painted canvas juxtaposed with printed matter, a taxidermied eagle, and a pillow tied with cord, hanging by a hook from the picture. In such works, viewers are provoked to physically, visually, and semantically wander around an expanse that may exude devotional qualities, but does not cohere or concentrate upon a singular subject, either conceptually or compositionally. As Anna Dezeuze has pointed out, Cornell and Rauschenberg did share an attraction to dime-store items, souvenirs, and popular magazines—enacting the concepts of accumulation and repetition that make up the dynamics of shopping and collecting.[58] For both artists, recurring imagery and repeated photographs expressed the idea of obsessive fixation on specific images and products. These collecting practices reflected a tension between secrecy and display. But unlike Cornell, Rauschenberg wanted to maintain an "open" stance and to "collaborate" with objects: his surfaces are receptacles for detritus whose material qualities are further highlighted by being pasted, creased, or covered with paint. To some extent, this activity was associated with the arbitrary, a giving up of authorial control and stable identity. As Rauschenberg once stated: "The only difference between me and Cornell is that he puts his work behind glass, and mine is out in the world [...] He packed objects away, and I was unpacking them."[59] Rauschenberg strayed from the compartmentalizing device of the box in favor of what Leo Steinberg would call "the flatbed picture plane," a surface that acts as a receptacle for diverse and disjunctive assemblages of objects, materials, and imagery.[60] Consistently incorporating gestural and abstract painted passages into his relatively large works, Rauschenberg sought a more direct *bodily* confrontation with the viewer. His conglomerations of non-precious materials come across as more *monumental* in effect and yet often still human-scaled.

As with Rauschenberg's Combines, *tainted goods* works exhibit a complex and complicated relationship to cultures of the monument. In 1979, Rosalind Krauss made the convincing case that sculpture had its own set of rules which are not really that open to change. She argued that the logic of sculpture is inseparable from the logic of the monument—and is always in some sense a commemorative representation: "It sits in a particular place and speaks in a symbolic tongue about the meaning or use of that place."[61] As Buchloh has observed, sculpture, on the one hand, had been positioned within the mystical domain of the public sphere where it received the traditional placement and function of the monument, especially under the "flourishing memory industry of public and official assignments of commemoration."[62] On the other hand, it existed semiotically in the equally mythical but more powerfully "real" dimension of a world of industrially produced "signs." "Sculpture" had become associated with the fiction of an immediately accessible public space and a promise to provide instant acts of commemoration. For Buchloh, beginning in the 1960s "the conception of sculpture responds more systematically to the radical transformation of the object—and publicity—conditions in a society of advanced and enforced consumption ..." While Surrealist assemblage practices featured outdated commodities arranged in order to set free sudden insights of mnemonic experience, under more advanced capitalist conditions this mnemonic potential evaporated from objects under an artificially enforced and accelerated obsolescence. In the work of Claes Oldenburg and others during this time, this development may be seen in terms of a shift from *disjunctive* contexts of sculptural display to practices of *accumulation* depicting like objects, such as the assortment of found and unwanted materials—all arranged in the form of ray guns—housed in Oldenburg's legendary *Ray Gun Wing* from the 1970s, recently restaged at MoMA. For Buchloh, this lack of diversity makes the universalized conditions of fetishization apparent, and the disappearance of experience tied to knowledge of use value, along with any corresponding sense of the temporality and intimacy for the objects involved.

Drawing on alternative histories of assemblage—rather than on sculptural accumulations of the kind that Buchloh emphasizes above—I wish to explore the *continued* potential for temporal, pneumonic, and empathetic viewing experiences when confronting tainted goods works, which stage a critical (and often satirical) relationship to cultures of the monument and the memorial, and to a range of museological traditions, while simultaneously referring to domestic, retail, and other contexts. The sculptural displays addressed in this book continue to play with the notion of the promise of historical insight, within presentations that are never fully voided of mnemonic and therapeutic capacities, despite the undeniable devolution of museum spaces, which have degenerated from being places of public historical experience and self-definition into branches of the memory industry.[63] While acknowledging the current predicament of losing simultaneous collective experience, I choose to continue "pretending" (as Buchloh would perhaps put it) that forms of social and cultural critique can still happen within certain *staged* environments made up mostly of sculptural means.

Face It, You're a Formalist: Allow the Abstraction

The notion of *merely* playing or pretending is integral to my methodological approach. Indeed, in some sense *Tainted Goods* runs against the grain of mainstream art history scholarship, given my focus on close, formally attentive readings which prioritize associations experienced first-hand in the gallery; on the historical roots of recent assemblage; and on structural qualities that the works share, traits which transcend the (often) presumed divide between the modern and the contemporary. As James Elkins has argued, the current state of art history has entered a period of high competency and strikingly low stakes.[64] Researchers are obliged to delve into the specificities of objects, with little or no interest in their impact on larger contexts (i.e., impact that may require a reframing and/or questioning of assumptions underlying the field). Johanna Burton has recently commented on Pamela Lee's scholarship as trying (with much success) to meet the challenge of accounting for contemporary art as it becomes historical—or that understands how the present is always already historical.[65] Like Lee, I aspire to embrace this difficulty, incorporating it into an account of assemblage practices that stubbornly resist being interpreted or historicized into neat and digestible packages, as knowledge that may be efficiently *mobilized* (to use a term popular lately among funding agencies).[66]

Charting a course through their respective works, I discuss how Farmer, Genzken, Harrison, and Magor alter consumer products, but never dissolve or mask then completely: the procedures exerted on them may be meant to subvert, in part, display strategies that rely on strategies of the seamless. I point to their preferences for fragmentary and abused objects, which seem to be straining within a predicament that resists the motives of their original production, advertisement, and sale. Accordingly, they engage in a critical dialogue with design-and-display cultures that strive to erase border zones between products and their promotion as images. These displays are, in a partial sense, resistant to institutional standards associated with the efficient exercise of historical contextualization and the education of the public. They cannot be easily reduced to bullet points in a curatorial argument. These artists' assemblage strategies engage in social and political critique, but never in didactic or dogmatic ways. The ambivalence is further complicated by a sense of the arbitrary, associated with the idea of *only arranging* objects, like toys and pieces of rope, as a display that is akin to retail shop window, rather than providing properly crafted works that are worthy of aesthetic contemplation in the traditional sense. Indeed, these practices maintain the importance—or at least the insistence—of everything that seems somehow unfit for exhibition. They court with a condition of travesty, often displaying absurd stand-ins for human beings: these "figures" act as place holders, rather than as receptacles for definitive, efficiently communicable meanings that are firmly planted in stone.

When experienced in succession within an exhibition, their works become productively unhinged from forms of critique dedicated definitively to any particular moment or individual agent. They exceed any attempts at reduction to a specific satirical or polemical argument about, say, imperialism and greed. Literal and abstract elements are slapped together, thus complicating any gestures toward characterization and personification, these being conventional requirements for monumental statements and pedagogical narratives. I am primarily interested in kinds of juxtaposition that encourage the viewer to actively project, and to consider contexts of capitalist consumption in which we are all, in some way, complicit. It is this form of projection, corresponding to a close encounter with the objects on hand, that *allows for abstraction* or a kind of *conceptual flexibility* which contributes to the epistemological importance of tainted goods—as a discourse that has the critical potential to resist (always in a partial way) prescriptive and doctrinal modes of thinking.

My understanding of this potential derives in part from my own scholarly training in formalist, feminist, and Marxist approaches to the historical and neo-avant-gardes, including (post)conceptual and (post)minimal practices that share a pronounced concern with process combined with expressions of difference (in terms of gender, ethnicity, and class) in relatively metaphorical ways, displayed with means that incorporate abstraction. These means allow for material and formal elements to take on lives of their own, and resist, in a partial sense, efficient circulation as signifiers of packaged identities, offered up as "research" with currency. In the late 1990s, the Whitney Independent Study Program provided me with a grounding in conceptual art, critical theory, psychoanalysis, and cultural studies; among other things, that experience provoked me into moving away from an exclusive focus on modernist studies to the study of recent art in historical ways. At the time, I felt fortunate to have already been schooled in an old-school sort of way, as a modernist steeped in formalist and iconographical methods, knowing that it is artworks—in all of their material and formal complexity—that would continue to be the starting point interpretively. A few years before participating in the Whitney ISP, I had read Yve-Alain Bois's book *Painting as Model* (1993), which motivated me to practice a form of art writing that is theoretically informed and yet resistant to the imperative of "applying" theory in an instrumentalizing fashion: to do so would be "a symptom of intellectual blackmail, a concession to the demands of the university's market."[67] Indeed, as a doctoral student at the CUNY Graduate Center during the 1990s, I was encouraged—in courses with Carol Armstrong and Jack Flam, among others—to develop interpretive and descriptive methods that would do justice to objects which combine figural and abstract elements, which are semantically and compositionally complex, and which are potentially prone to structural readings. Influenced by a methodological seminar on formalisms with Carol, I eventually wrote a dissertation on the history of formalist art history in German-speaking countries (a more academic topic would be hard to imagine).[68] Another source that played a formative role was Krauss's *The Optical Unconscious* (1993).[69] The post-structural and psychological qualities of Krauss's account—which crucially combined close readings of modernist and postwar works—served for me as a shining example of what art history and criticism could be. But it was Carol's teaching and writing in particular that most helped to shape my core interest in striving to describe well—while accounting for my own interpretive subjectivity in a measured sense—hopefully in ways that are productive and provocative for the reader.

Notes

1 In different ways, these exhibitions offer gaps between images and referents that create the potential for a crossing of semantic switches, or a perceptual friction that generates cognitive sparks and insights. I borrow some of my terms here from Susan Buck-Morss's classic work *The Dialectics of Seeing: Walter Benjamin and the Arcades Project* (Cambridge, MA: MIT Press, 1989).

2 With reference to Krauss's influence, Johanna Burton has discussed distinctions between sculpture and installation art works that are particularly helpful to my project, critically taking into account spectacular installation practices which reflect the phenomenon of "today's foregrounding of the audience [which] produces not individual bodies with differences but, rather, an interchangeable public, or *mass*." With Burton, I think that it is useful to focus on sculptural traditions that are not installations. See Burton, "Sculpture: Not-Not-Not (Or, Pretty Liar)," in Anne Ellegood, ed., *The Uncertainty of Objects and Ideas: Recent Sculpture* (Washington, DC: Hirshhorn Museum and Sculpture Garden, 2006), 10–17.

3 Krauss, "Sculpture in the Expanded Field" (1979), in Hal Foster, ed., *The Anti-Aesthetic: Essays on Postmodern Culture* (New York: New Press, 1983), 35–47.

4 See Foster, "The Crux of Minimalism" (1986), in *The Return of the Real: The Avant-Garde at the End of the Century* (Cambridge, MA: MIT Press, 1996), 34–68. In this regard, I also recall Thomas McEvilley's treatment of the move beyond the traditional sculptural object and the

freeing up of boundaries between media, one that in recent years has generally degenerated into uncritical phenomena, "... just one further wonder of the triumph of late capitalism" (4). McEvilley emphasizes a formative phase in the 1960s, when there existed a genuine tension between an open intervention into three-dimensional space and an awareness of a work's resistant object-likeness and "troublesome facticity": the "work didn't disclose itself to the viewer with quite the same ease as painting or image-based work—its inert thingness, its impinging on the viewer's space, still getting in the way of normative patterns of visual consumption" (4). I wish to situate these critical qualities within recent assemblage-based practices. See McEvilley, *Sculpture in the Age of Doubt* (New York: Allworth Press, 1999), 4.

5   See Bishop, *Artificial Hells: Participatory Art and the Politics of Spectatorship* (London: Verso, 2012), 275–77. See also, as cited by Bishop, Jodi Dean, *Democracy and Other Neoliberal Fantasies: Communicative Capitalism and Left Politics* (Durham, NC: Duke University Press, 2009), 13.

6   Bishop's critique of Antony Gormley's *One and the Other* (2009) is particularly relevant to some of my arguments. Gormley's project allowed people to occupy the empty "Fourth Plinth" of Trafalgar Square, one hour at a time for 100 days; the plinth's occupants were continuously streamed online. "In a world where everyone can air their views to everyone we are faced not with mass empowerment but with an endless stream of egos levelled to banality. Far from being oppositional to spectacle, participation has now entirely merged with it." See Bishop, *Artificial Hells*, 277.

7   Relevant in this regard are Alex Potts's discussions of how the process of commodification may threaten sculpture's critical capabilities within the large-scale museum context. Its potential resistance runs up against the disintegrating drive of an increasingly pervasive and unrestricted process of commodification, consumption, and capital accumulation—a system that constantly erodes any fixed mediations between the individual and public arena. See Potts, *The Sculptural Imagination: Figurative, Modernist, Minimalist* (New Haven: Yale University Press, 2000).

8   Indeed, slides are "apparatuses that induce a repetitive kinetic pleasure" and may serve as an outlet for discharging "surplus" energy, wearing us out so that we do not cause problems. For comments on the notion of "fear as pleasure" as it pertains to the history of slides, see Roy Kozlovsky, "A Short History of Slides," in *Carsten Höller: Test Site* (London: Tate Modern, 2006), 44–45.

9   See Jessica Morgan, "Turbine Höller," in *Carsten Höller: Test Site*, 11–15.

10 For discussion of playground atmospheres and "childish joy" in relation to Höller's work, see Dorothea von Hantelmann, "I," in *Carsten Höller: Test Site*, 33, 19. For some mention of Pine and Gilmore's book, see Hantelmann, "Von der Anti-Ästhetik zur ästhetischen Erfahrung," *Texte zur Kunst* 81 (March 2011): 94–120.

11 Horkheimer and Adorno, *Dialectic of Enlightenment*, trans. J. Cumming (New York: Continuum, 1982), 139–40. See Weitzman, "No Fun: Aporias of Pleasure in Adorno's Aesthetic Theory," *The German Quarterly* 81, no. 2 (Spring 2008): 185–202.

12 See Adorno, *Aesthetic Theory*, trans. R. Hullot-Kentor (Minneapolis: University of Minnesota Press, 1997), 135–36, 311: "Because all happiness found in the status quo is ersatz and false, art must break its promise in order to stay true to it."

13 See Foster, *Design and Crime, and Other Diatribes* (London: Verso, 2002).

14 "For today you don't have to be filthy rich to be projected not only as designer but as designed – whether the product in question is your home or your business, your sagging face (designer surgery) or your lagging personality (designer drugs), your historical memory (designer museums) or your DNA structure (designer children)." For Foster, this is analogous to postmodernism's "constructed subject."

15 See www.tate.org.uk/whats-on/tate-modern/exhibition/unilever-series-rachel-whiteread-embankment/rachel-whiteread (last accessed April 12, 2018).

16 Revised edition (Boston: Harvard Business Review, 2011).

17 On this notion of "being watched," see especially Paul Woodruff, *The Necessity of Theatre: The Art of Watching and Being Watched* (New York: Oxford University Press, 2008).

18 Pine and Gilmore, 240, 254–55.

19 Ibid., 77.

20 Ibid., 142.

21 Massimiliano Gioni, Gary Carrion-Murayari, and Jenny Moore, eds., *Carsten Höller: Experience* (New York: New Museum and Skira Rizzoli, 2011), 39–41. I should mention that I have great admiration for much of Höller's practice, and have previously (and quite favorably) interpreted several of his major installations. See for instance my review of his large-scale exhibition at Shawinigan Space, Quebec, in *Artforum* (November 2007).

22 Ibid., 53–55.

23 The catalogue is chock-full of unintentionally ironic, forced, and apprehensive commentary, as in the case of a conversation with the artist that is focused on Duchamp's importance, even though Gioni admits in his introduction that Höller and Duchamp have little in common. I also was curious to find Hal Foster's rather diplomatic posing of a series of questions, as if he were not quite convinced of Höller's critical capabilities, particularly within the context of a blockbuster survey show: "Can an artist deploy confusion and doubt effectively today? What does it mean to bring the fairground and playground into the space of the museum?" (229).

24 In its avoidance of apocalyptic and totalizing conceptions of spectacle, my argument in some ways bears similarities to Jörg Heiser, *All of a Sudden: Things that Matter in Contemporary Art* (Berlin: Sternberg Press, 2010).

25 Centered on the synchronic, structuralists have studied such phenomena artificially, under ahistorical conditions—neglecting the historical contexts out of which they have emerged. But structuralists have of course always recognized this artifice, and the idea that their discourse can and should only be defined in terms of differences between it and diachronic interpretations, including biographical ones. For a useful, summarizing discussion, see Jonathan Culler, *Structuralist Poetics: Structuralism, Linguistics, and the Study of Literature* (London: Routledge & Kegan Paul, 1975), 230–38. For

perceptive commentary, see Frederic Jameson's classic work, *The Prison-House of Language: A Critical Account of Structuralism and Russian Formalism* (Princeton: Princeton University Press, 1972). Jameson discusses structuralism's rejection of the ego, and dissolution of the subject into sheer relationality, reflecting a "distorted awareness of the dawning collective character of life, as a kind of blurred reflection of the already collective structure of what is perhaps less cybernetic than the mass-production commercial network into which our individual existences are organized" (196). I am grateful to Ron Clark for first introducing me to Jameson's early work long ago, when I was a critical studies fellow in the Whitney Independent Study Program.

26 See Didi-Huberman, *Confronting Images: Questioning the Ends of a Certain History of Art* (1990), trans. John Goodman (University Park, PA: Penn State University Press, 2005), 140–43, 140.

27 Ibid., 159–60. This process is further informed by Russian formalist studies of poetic language as a dialect that, in the words of Jameson, "attracts attention to itself, and such attention results in renewed perception of the very material quality of language itself." See Jameson, *The Prison-House of Language*, 50, 61, 70.

28 Isabelle Graw has recently discussed the anthropomorphizing aspects of both Harrison and Genzken's works, in which objects are forced into playing human roles in obviously inadequate ways; this procedure's inadequacy may alternate between tragic and absurd connotations. But it is their consistent inclusion of abstract material that signifies the crucial disconnect between consumer goods and human identity. See Graw, "Ecce Homo," *Artforum* 50, no. 3 (November 2011): 241–47. I am grateful to Isabelle Graw for helpful comments and participation in a session I co-chaired on recent sculpture at the College Art Association Conference, New York, 2011.

29 For excellent commentary, see Anna McMullan, *Performing Embodiment in Samuel Beckett's Drama* (New York: Routledge, 2010), 110, 31–44, 105–30. Werner Spies suggests that "in general, much of what minimalism offers is grounded in Beckett's visual abstinence." See Spies, "Image Afterwards: An After Word," in Breon Mitchell and Lois Overbeck, eds., *Samuel Beckett and the Visual Text* (Atlanta: Emory University Press, 1999), 55. And see the catalogue *Samuel Beckett/Bruce Nauman* (Vienna: Vienna Kunsthalle, 2000).

30 See Agnes Heller, *Immortal Comedy: The Comic Phenomenon in Art, Literature, and Life* (Oxford: Lexington Books, 2005).

31 The ironist and humanist are "singular" beings, as Kierkegaard points out, and can only exist in societies that tolerate a space for individual freedom of judgment and for playing around with normative ideas (not necessarily political freedom), testing and suspending everyday and scientific uncertainties. See Søren Kierkegaard, *The Concept of Irony with Constant Reference to Socrates*, trans. L. M. Capel (New York: Harper & Row, 1965), 260.

32 See Rancière, *The Emancipated Spectator*, trans. Gregory Elliot (London: Verso, 2009), 21, 22.

33 For interesting discussion of Rancière's discourse in relation to recent sculptural practices, see the Introduction to Eva Grubinger and Jörg Heiser, eds.,
Sculpture Unlimited (Berlin: Sternberg Press, 2011).

34 Ibid. The "ontology of the dissensual is actually a fictional ontology, a play
of 'aesthetic ideas'. The set of relations that constitutes the work operates
as if it had a different ontological texture from the sensations that make up
everyday experience" (67).

35 Ibid., 72–73, 75. The artwork does not frame a collective body, but
encourages a multiplicity of "connections and disconnections that reframe
the relation between bodies, the world they live in, and the way in which
they are equipped to adapt to it. It is a multiplicity of folds and gaps in the
fabric of common experience that change the cartography of the percep-
tible, the thinkable, and the feasible. As such it allows for new modes of
political construction of common objects and new possibilities of collective
enunciation."

36 As James Meyer has discussed, massively spectacular installation practices
do not really encourage productive and critical reflection on the conditions
of their display, but rather help to affirm those conditions. With Meyer,
I want to advocate for sculptural experiences that are *somatic* in the sense
that they have a scale and other qualities capable of inducing a more active
and human-scaled awareness. See Meyer, "No More Scale," *Artforum* 42,
no. 10 (Summer 2004): 220–28.

37 See Fried, *Art and Objecthood: Essays and Reviews* (Chicago: University
of Chicago Press, 1998), 128; and Rebentisch, *Aesthetics of Installation
Art* (2003), trans. D. Hendrickson with G. Jackson (Berlin: Sternberg
Press, 2012), 52. Rebentisch's is among the most important philosophical
and critical treatments of the installation art genre. My study obviously
differs from hers in many ways, including its focus on detailed analysis of
individual works and in its rejection of the "installation art" category in
favor of sculpture. Another crucial account—rare in its offering of aesthetic theorizations, comparative discussions, and critical commentary—
is Claire Bishop, *Installation Art: A Critical History* (London: Tate
Publishing, 2005).

38 See Didi-Huberman, *Ce que nous voyons, ce qui nous regarde* (Paris: Editions
de minuit, 1992), 58–59, 115.

39 Rebentisch, *Aesthetics of Installation Art*, 262–71. Simple identification
with the work should be undermined, compelling us to have a performative
and self-reflective dialogue that reflects our own baggage of cultural and
social assumptions. Hence, the meanings that come to appear in the work
may never be truly warranted by the work—and so we each have to reflect
on our own productivity in the creation of relations of meaning.

40 A particularly important recent source in this regard—based on conference
proceedings—is Isabelle Graw, Daniel Birnbaum, and Nikolaus Hirsch, eds.,
Art and Subjecthood: The Return of the Human Figure in Semiocapitalism
(Berlin: Sternberg Press, 2011). Some of my aesthetic criteria are similar to
those mentioned by Anne Ellegood in the catalogue for the innovative exhibition *The Uncertainty of Objects and Ideas: Recent Sculpture* (Washington,
DC: Hirshhorn Museum and Sculpture Garden, 2006), 18–29.

41 In this regard, I am indebted to David Joselit's discussion of Rachel Harrison's works in terms of hurtful effects. Harrison employs defacement (a wig on a Franz West sculpture) and social satire (a "slave" carries a president's head under her arm), qualities which can come across as hurtful when they are put in motion and given an agency that may be wholly unexpected, and therefore all-the-more powerful in effect. She "extracts the social skin from bodies, externalizing it in masks, wigs, and garments, and then lets it slip, exposing an embarrassing nakedness—something we don't wish to see ..." See Joselit, "Touch to Begin ..." in Eric Banks and Sarah Valdez, eds., *Rachel Harrison: Museum With Walls* (Annandale on Hudson, London, and Frankfurt: Center for Curatorial Studies, Bard College; Whitechapel Gallery; and Portikus, 2010), 198.

42 Some of my language here is indebted to Josiah McElheny's insightful text, "Readymade Resistance: On Art and the Forms of Industrial Production," *Artforum* (October 2007): 327–35. See also Mary Ceruti, et al., *Where is Production? Inquiries into Contemporary Sculpture* (London and New York: SculptureCenter and Black Dog Publishing, 2013).

43 See especially David Joselit, "Touch to Begin ..." and Jack Bankowsky, "Monkey House Blessing Potpourri," in Eric Banks and Sarah Valdez, eds., *Rachel Harrison: Museum With Walls*, 186–99, 136–47. Bankowsky comments on Harrison's relationship to the Combines, pointing out that her compositional elements—everything from pure paint to tabloid drivel—do not, relatively speaking, "really come together ... They coexist," hence encouraging thought right at the edge of meaninglessness or legibility (140). Similarly, Joselit helpfully discusses how Harrison resists fully absorbing readymade objects within a composition or revising their grammar; rather she "host[s] them in a liminal state where association is both promiscuous and obscure." See also Rachel Harrison and Eric Banks, "Hostess with the Mostess," in Darsie Alexander, ed., *Franz West: To Build a House You Start with the Roof: Work 1972–2008* (Cambridge, MA and Baltimore: MIT Press and Baltimore Museum of Art, 2008), 172–85.

44 Gioni, "Ask the Dust," in *Unmonumental: The Object in the 21st Century* (London and New York: Phaidon and New Museum, 2007), 65. The co-curator of the exhibition, Laura Hoptman, concisely describes the process of juxtaposition in unmonumental works that employ already-made parts, pieces, or entire objects that retain their identities even as they function together as a single work. Each part could be read for what it was and participate in the overall meaning of the whole. Compositional elements are incapable of mixing or attaining homogeneity. See Hoptman, "Unmonumental: Going to Pieces in the 21st Century," 128–39.

45 See ibid., Smith, "Sculpture: A Minor Place," 184–90, 185. Indeed, Smith mentions how one physically moves around unmonumental works but never through them; they exude a quality of embodiment combined with a curiously "withholding, indeterminate relationship to the viewer. With no overt figuration, bodies tend to be implied through close volumetric or structural comparison between object and viewing subject. And there is a shared distaste for high design values."

46 Some other relevant exhibitions (and accompanying publications) include Stephanie Rosenthal, Antje Longhi, and Isabella Kredler, eds., *Dinge in der Kunst des XX.* Jahrhunderts (Munich and Göttingen: Haus der Kunst and Steidl Verlag, 2000); "Part Object/Part Sculpture" (Wexner Center, 2005); *Gone Formalism* (ICA, Philadelphia, 2006); and *Abstract Resistance* (Walker Art Centre, 2010). See also Kasper König and Thomas D. Trummer, et al., *Before the Law: Postwar Sculptures and Spaces of Contemporary Art* (Cologne: Museum Ludwig and Verlag der Buchhandlung Walter König, 2012). For some perceptive commentary, see Diedrich Diedrichsen's review of "Before the Law" in *Artforum* (April 2012).

47 For commentary see, for instance, Roger Shattuck, "Introduction: How Collage Became Assemblage," in John Elderfield, ed., *Essays on Assemblage: Studies in Modern Art 2* (New York: Museum of Modern Art, 1992), 119–23.

48 See Seitz, *The Art of Assemblage* (New York: Museum of Modern Art, 1961), 116–17, 134.

49 See Walker Percy, "Metaphor as Mistake," in *The Message in the Bottle* (New York: Farrar, Straus, 1975).

50 For insightful observations, see Walter Hopps, *Kienholz: A Retrospective* (New York: Whitney Museum of American Art, 1996), 74, 87.

51 Seitz, *The Art of Assemblage*, 86.

52 For helpful comments, see Ingrid Pfeiffer, "Temporary Objects: mannequins at the 1938 *Exposition international du surréalisme*," in Pfeiffer and Max Hollein, eds., *Surreal Objects: Three-Dimensional Works from Dali to Man Ray* (Frankfurt and Ostfildern: Schirn Kunsthalle Frankfurt and Hatje Cantz Verlag, 2011), 60–81.

53 For detailed discussion, see Annabelle Görgen, "Exposition international du surréalisme Paris 1938: Bluff und Täuschung – Die Ausstellung als Werk: Einflüsse aus dem 19. Jahrhundert unter dem Aspekt der Kohärenz" (diss., Braunschweig, Munich, 2008).

54 See Ulrich Lehmann, "The Surrealist Object and Subject in Materialism: Notes on the Understanding of the Object and Surrealism," in *Surreal Objects*, op. cit, 128–35.

55 See Benjamin, *Arcades Project*, ed. Wolf Tiedemann (Cambridge, MA: Harvard University Press, 1999), 206, 883–84.

56 See Buck-Morss, *The Dialectics of Seeing*, 67, 284.

57 See Buchloh, "Sculpture: Publicity and the Poverty of Experience," (1996) in Buchloh, *Formalism and Historicity* (Cambridge, MA: MIT Press, 2015), 509–28.

58 For excellent discussion see Dezeuze, "Unpacking Joseph Cornell: Consumption and Play in the Work of Robert Rauschenberg, Andy Warhol and George Brecht," in Jason Edwards and Stephanie Taylor, eds., *Joseph Cornell: Opening the Box* (Bern: Peter Lang, 2003), 219–42.

59 Quoted in Deborah Solomon, *Utopia Parkway: The Life and Work of Joseph Cornell* (New York: Farrar, Straus & Giroux, 1996), 237.

60 See Steinberg, "Reflections on the State of Art Criticism" (1972), reprinted in Brandon Joseph, ed., *Robert Rauschenberg* (Cambridge, MA: MIT Press, 2002), 27.

61 See Krauss, "Sculpture in the Expanded Field," *October* 8 (Spring 1979): 33.

62 See Buchloh, "Sculpture: Publicity and the Poverty of Experience," 522.

63 "In fact it makes evident to what degree the organization of history and the accumulation of commodity objects in the department store were evolving toward each other from the start that once an object had been isolated from its function and contexts and had been given over to exhibition value it would inevitably fuse with the condition of the isolated and fetishized commodity object as the central category of object experience." See Buchloh, "Sculpture: Publicity and the Poverty of Experience," 524.

64 See Elkins, *Master Narratives and Their Discontents* (New York: Routledge, 2005).

65 See Burton's Preface to Pamela M. Lee, *New Games: Postmodernism After Contemporary Art* (New York: Routledge, 2013), xv–xxviii.

66 I am striving, in a sense, to enact a methodological impossibility, one that is ostensibly infused with doubt. As Pamela Lee discusses, Jean-François Lyotard describes the status of contemporary knowledge relative to its performativity in a pertinent way: "Knowledge is and will be produced in order to be sold … consumed in order to be valorized in a new production: in both cases, the goal is exchange." As Lee puts it, "rationalization of knowledge as information—as so much fodder for the market—has a decisive effect on what we do as art historians and how we proceed in the most seemingly mundane fashion." See Lee, *New Games*, 15; and Lyotard, *The Postmodern Condition: A Report on Knowledge*, trans. Brian Massumi (Minneapolis: University of Minnesota Press, 1984), 4.

67 See Bois, "Resisting Blackmail," in *Painting as Model* (Cambridge, MA: MIT Press, 1993), xii.

68 Of particular interest were Armstrong's books *Scenes in a Library: Reading the Photograph in the Book, 1843–1875* (Cambridge, MA: MIT Press, 1998) and *Manet/Manette* (New Haven: Yale University Press, 2002).

69 Cambridge, MA: MIT Press, 1993. These aspects of Krauss's book were critically discussed and debated at length in a seminar with Benjamin Buchloh that I attended at Columbia University. I only realized later how much of an effect that debate had on my choices of research focus and methodological position.

1   Rachel Harrison
"Consider the Lobster"

Entering Rachel Harrison's exhibition "Consider the Lobster," I am greeted by a gridded bulletin board, hanging on an otherwise bare beige wall.[1] It is, in fact, a chart, containing dozens of little labels, printed with names and job titles. People are grouped according to categories: the boroughs of New York City, "Home Attendant," "Continuing Treatment," and "Supportive Employment." It may have been a psychiatric hospital's means of organizing duty assignments, a bureaucratic instrument identified with the mental health services of a specific city.[2] I speculate on its symbolic scope—as a cross-section of a massive metropolitan milieu, a facilitating means of designating people who treat (or process) those who are marginalized, those who are habitually labeled as different, abnormal, or as not leading productive and useful lives, those who are obsolete (or at risk of becoming so) and therefore considered a burden on the rest of society. Obviously referencing pre-digital technologies, this object is infused with a sense of obsolescence. The tiny cards register as actual documentation of individuals while, in a more metaphorical sense, represent a spectrum of vocations: social workers, nurses, records analysts, rehab techs, psychiatrists, counselors, porters, financial managers, clerks. Taken from its original context (a hospital's offices), it now forms part of Harrison's installation *Snake in the Grass* (1997/2009). It inspires speculation partly because it is not anchored by any established traditions of iconography—either in terms of art or popular culture—such as romanticizing treatments of the mentally ill or the exploitive spectacles of degraded, down-and-out humanity.

I am struck by the starkness of this chart, so prominently placed in the show, as an artifact signifying mental health problems permeating a population. It offers an unusual invitation to consider how and why so many of us struggle to cope with pressures and insecurities. Webster's defines a "snake in the grass" as a thing or person that is seemingly harmless and helpful—or one posing as a positive influence—but that is secretly faithless, capable of treachery and much harm. The snake in the grass notion may be situated within cultures of consumerism,

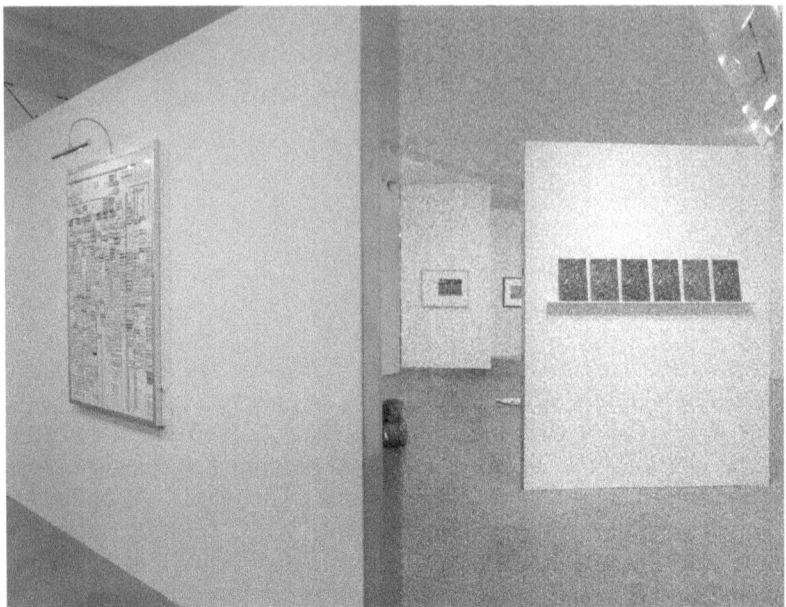

Figure 1.1 Rachel Harrison, *Snake in the Grass*, 1997/2009

Installation view, "Consider the Lobster," curated by Tom Eccles, Center for Curatorial Studies, Bard College, Annandale-on-Hudson, New York, June 27 – December 20, 2009

Polystyrene, acrylic, aluminum studs, Sheetrock, rope, garbage bags, La Gloria Cubana cigar, baking tray, olive pits, shovel, snakeskin, Rock Box cooler, foam art-handling blocks, FEGS hospital chart, wood, picture lamp, exit sign, bottled water, ten chromogenic prints, and one pigmented inkjet print

138 × 288 × 498 inches (350.5 × 731.5 × 1264.9 cm)

Courtesy of the artist and Greene Naftali, New York. Photo: Jason Mandella

saturating our spaces of work and play. Increasingly, these cultures are expressed as "packaged" experiences, promising fulfillment but failing to deliver the goods. Partly in response to such failure, we may develop neurotic and depressive behaviors, particularly when what is commonly categorized as "fun" does little to alleviate the malaise. The cultural critic David Foster Wallace certainly suffered from such symptoms. In the article "Consider the Lobster"—also the title of Harrison's exhibition—he muses about forms of tourist entertainment in America that commercialize authentic local flavor, such as a lobster festival in New England:

To be a mass tourist, for me, is to become a pure late-date American: alien, ignorant, greedy for something you cannot ever have, disappointed in a way that you can never admit … It is, in lines and gridlock and transaction after transaction, to confront a dimension of yourself that is as inescapable as it is painful: As a tourist, you become economically significant but existentially loathsome, an insect or a dead thing.[3]

Harrison does choose a tourist destination as a subject in *Snake in the Grass*: the site of the JFK assassination in Dallas. Moving beyond the introductory chart on the beige wall, I find a photo offering a partial view of a famous image—shot moments after the fatal shot(s) were taken—of a policeman sprinting across a grassy patch of ground, passing picnicking people, toward the Grassy Knoll. Harrison provides a photograph of this legendary picture, perhaps purchased in Dallas: her work includes a $20 yellow price tag, as well as a fragment of text that mentions a key witness to the assassination, Beverly Oliver. Another photo shows a grinning and aproned man, holding a souvenir photo depicting a bird's-eye view of Kennedy's motorcade route; the top of this picture's frame serves as a resting place for a Mi Cubano cigar—a punning gesture that may reflect a Cuba-related, conspiracy-laden conversation with the depicted man. However, in the gallery there are other photographs of individuals who are just hanging around. Not composed with care, these latter images were presumably taken around the Grassy Knoll area—souvenirs from trips taken to the tragic site: one depicts two men on the grass; their faces are not revealed, and they stand awkwardly, with arms at their sides, perhaps struggling to come up with meanings that satisfy or fulfill. Another shows a man in profile, with a blank expression. Considered independently, these images fail to deliver discernible events that could function as evidence of being anywhere; they are not even suitable for posting on Facebook or Instagram.

Normally "JFK" is a character cast in terms of tragically unfulfilled promises: of social reform, of progressive government, of glamor and intrigue (Marilyn and mob ties). Harrison may be implying that the Kennedy Camelot is a fantasy that many of us just prefer to rub up against, in a nostalgia-infused daze, as one literally lingers on a patch of grass—rather than face the realities of present-day politics. Indeed, on a shelf fastened to one wall, Harrison has lined up six close-up photographs of grass—according to Harrison, they were taken on the Grassy Knoll—rendered in different shades of green; the images might reflect the repetitive, and perhaps neurotic, investigative intent of looking for traces of evidence, or they may indicate a mere testing of different printing processes. But they are also, quite simply, pictures of grass, on display here as consumer (non-)options or (anti-)products, relatives of Warhol's series of *Campbell's Soup Cans* (offered in 1962 as multiple flavors on shelves, like those in in grocery-store aisles).

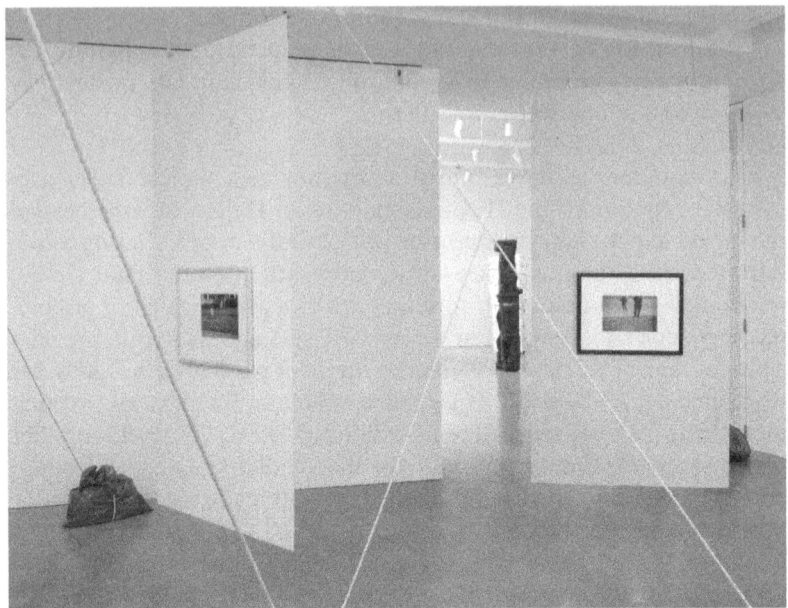

Figure 1.2 Rachel Harrison, *Snake in the Grass*, 1997/2009
Installation view, "Consider the Lobster," curated by Tom Eccles, Center for
Curatorial Studies, Bard College, Annandale-on-Hudson, New York, June 27 –
December 20, 2009
Polystyrene, acrylic, aluminum studs, Sheetrock, rope, garbage bags, La Gloria
Cubana cigar, baking tray, olive pits, shovel, snakeskin, Rock Box cooler, foam
art-handling blocks, FEGS hospital chart, wood, picture lamp, exit sign, bottled
water, ten chromogenic prints, and one pigmented inkjet print
138 × 288 × 498 inches (350.5 × 731.5 × 1264.9 cm)
Courtesy of the artist and Greene Naftali, New York. Photo: Jason Mandella

   And, quite crucially, all of Harrison's images have been placed upon
pseudo walls, either hanging from the ceiling or held in place precariously with the aid of bright yellow ropes and forest-green garbage bags
filled with unknown (presumably heavy) material. While it is intriguing
to think of refuse as the supportive substance for Harrison's exhibition
design, the bags and ropes help to facilitate a speculative, sculptural
stage for viewing. I wander and wonder about what, who, and where
the worthy content is. But one thing is certain: that I have strayed from
a seamlessly packaged, nostalgia-soaked, tourist experience about the
death of a president. The yellow lines of rope occur at assertively diag-
onal angles across the space; they must be acknowledged, along with
those precarious "walls," as display surfaces here divorced from the

notion of load-bearing, monumental architecture. Any centered sense of self-awareness, of a clear-cut narrative, is further complicated by considering the material realities of twine, drywall, and green plastic—along with the activities of suspending, hoisting, spanning, and extending—as subjects in themselves. Sheetrock and aluminum studs are exposed, along with an array of miscellaneous things that help the installation resist being cast as a conventionally museological, tourist experience: water bottles for offices (perhaps belonging to Bard or a hospital?); a bundle of wooden slats; a brand-new "Rock Box" cooler placed upon its cardboard container (suitable for a luncheon on a Grassy Knoll?); along with shipping paraphernalia that may speak to the processing, installation, and transport of (art) goods. On the floor lies a baking tray; instead of cookies, Harrison has scattered olive pits resembling animal droppings. Nearby is a snow shovel, with a green scoop serving as a tray of sorts, offering up a decaying, neatly rolled-up snakeskin: another snake in the grass.

Combining an incoherent range of references to JFK, the Dealey Plaza area, and a lot more, Harrison's display does not serve up senti-mentalizing entertainment. There are no heroes to empathize with, no nostalgic flavors to enjoy. The tour guide is replaced by hangers-on, stum-bling around. The meandering installation expresses the divide between our selves and history, and operates in tension with narratives designed for spoon-fed consumption, about villains and heroic protagonists (e.g., Jim Garrison, as portrayed in Oliver Stone's film *JFK*). And yet her work strikes deeply ambivalent notes, wavering between an indis-criminately curious pursuit of experience (i.e., just hanging out at the Grassy Knoll, staring with your camera at the grass), morbid fantasy (about sensational, violent death), and conspiracy lore (organized crime, anti-Castro Cubans, the CIA, and Texas oilmen). Harrison's approach depends on the role that photographic experience plays in facilitating such fictions and fantasies, allowing them to stray from offi-cial accounts. The American brand of cultural enlightenment is so often based on the re-living or re-creation of tragic events. An assassination site becomes the object of fascination, a destination for history buffs or run-of-the-mill tourists, and a pilgrimage site for the purpose of reflec-tion, for those wishing to "share" in the collective mourning of a nation. Grief for a head of state may mellow like a fine wine over the decades, perhaps to be savored by those wishing to detect alternating hints of irony and sincerity. But in the end all that remains are trash bags, photos of grass, and olive pits. As with Wallace, Harrison's approach to the tourist experience is satirical and ironic in tone: suspicious of moral-izing conclusions—which shut down speculation and questioning—and those who tend to pronounce them, including museums.[4] One such institution is the Sixth Floor Museum—housed in the Texas School

Book Depository building—which employs hundreds of photographs, films, artifacts, and other hard evidence to educate tour groups about the assassination and its aftermath. In contrast, Harrison's satirical treatment is made possible in part through acts of indirect borrowing and mediation—as in the case of photos of parts of photos—reflecting a perspective that feels decentered and arbitrary.[5]

Worth recalling in this regard are Cady Noland's assemblages, which similarly satirized American mythologies, including those based on moments when a disastrous event became a spectacle, or when people are transformed into media icons. As in the case of her series of *Trashed Mailbox* and *Misc. Spill* works from the 1980s and early 1990s, Noland's practice did indeed develop in the wake of specific American events—the Vietnam War, the Kennedy assassinations, the brutal treatment of protestors at the 1968 Democratic Convention in Chicago, and Watergate—phenomena that threatened the country's image as a united, just, and invincible society. Like Harrison, Noland offered haphazard arrangements that combine iconic images (flags, celebrity photos, references to tabloids) with found objects that may initially seem unrelated, including those from the consumer world (grocery basket, shopping cart, beer cans), along with elements expressing the notions of repression, impairment, and debilitation (walkers, handcuffs, metal barricades). Crucially, only some of these components may be definitively identified with American contexts, and so the works manage to resonate in more dispersed and far-reaching ways. Unlike Harrison, however, Noland's works are often devoted in relatively focused ways to antiheroes with a cult status, like Oswald and Patty Hearst. Hearst's multiple personae, which ranged from fairy-tale princess to terrorist, were subject to media exploitation; transferring silkscreen enlargements of media imagery onto brushed aluminum supports, Noland portrayed her in these various guises in a manner that runs closer to the specificity of portraiture.

In *Snake in the Grass* the subject—the "main event"— may only be accessed indirectly, within a fragmented and disjointed formal frame, populated by "characters" and "artifacts" that seem utterly inadequate as informational sources or institutionally prescribed stories about what happened in Dallas, why it matters, and how we should remember it. The work reads best as a satirical statement, meant in part to provoke unexpected contemplation about the cultural motivations for delivering "JFK" as a packaged product, chock-full of national and sentimental pride. Indeed this may be a far more revealing and challenging "snake in the grass" to consider. As with much of "Consider the Lobster," I read Harrison's work as a conglomeration of fragments caught up in the process of losing currency, offering a display with tentative and tenuous authority, as infotainment or anything else.[6] It is crucial to consider the abstract and material qualities acquired by things when they lose their transmissibility and comprehensibility—the fraying edges of labels and hanging walls, the sheen of green trash bags, staring at the shoes of a couple of guys hanging around on the Grassy Knoll, only partly posing in the camera's sights—striking alternating notes of absurdity and alienation. It provokes reflection on our predicament, on our diminished capacity to make links between old and new, with confidence or assurance.[7] This lack is rooted in a culture of incessant accumulation, of products and experiences, which promise "currency" and fulfillment but never really deliver the goods.

Another of Harrison's installations, *Perth Amboy* (originally shown at Greene Naftali, New York, in the spring of 2001), lends itself to a similar process of questioning about the notions of currency and packaging. The room is filled with flimsy, folded pieces of cardboard, arranged as a maze-like configuration that encourages self-conscious wandering, not knowing whether jolting one of these makeshift barriers could spell disaster for the entire labyrinth. This sense of bodily awareness and tentativeness complicates any feelings of novelty felt when turning each corner to discover diverse products: multi-colored straws are stacked in a peripheral alcove. An aging bust of Marilyn Monroe—crudely adorned with orange hair—peers out from a Stor-All box, placed on a dolly with metal coasters. Junk-store trinkets and toys are situated in disparate parts of the maze on four pedestals. On one white plinth stands a doll in a wheelchair, accessorized with a camera, staring intently at a photograph of a freshly painted green wall. Harrison informed me that Becky, Barbie's handicapped pal, is no longer in production. Another pedestal is mirrored and supports a plastic toy family of Dalmatians, who face an envelope—crushed, torn, and placed upright so it seems monumental in relation to its canine viewers. Another salmon-pink pedestal has a weathered head of a Native-American chief, inscribed, strangely, with cave-writing motifs; with sunglasses nearby, he gazes at a small, wooden easel on which rests a framed photo of a sunset (with the sun going down, eyewear is no longer required). Standing on a black Formica base is an Asian ceramic scholar figure—still retaining its one-dollar price, scribbled in pencil on his heart. He gazed at a meteoric Styrofoam rock—indeed a natural monument—rendered in synthetic blue to match the figure's garb.

Harrison's display is comparable to a cardboard stage, upon which she presents acts of gazing, in its various guises; these acts may be seen as devotional or contemplative, often reflecting a sincere interest in pursuing knowledge, wonders, or enlightenment. But such sincerity is tainted by a keen sense of obsolescence: Harrison's props contribute a flavor of tragic comedy, suggested by toys and kitsch items that seem somehow inadequate as means to express "characters"

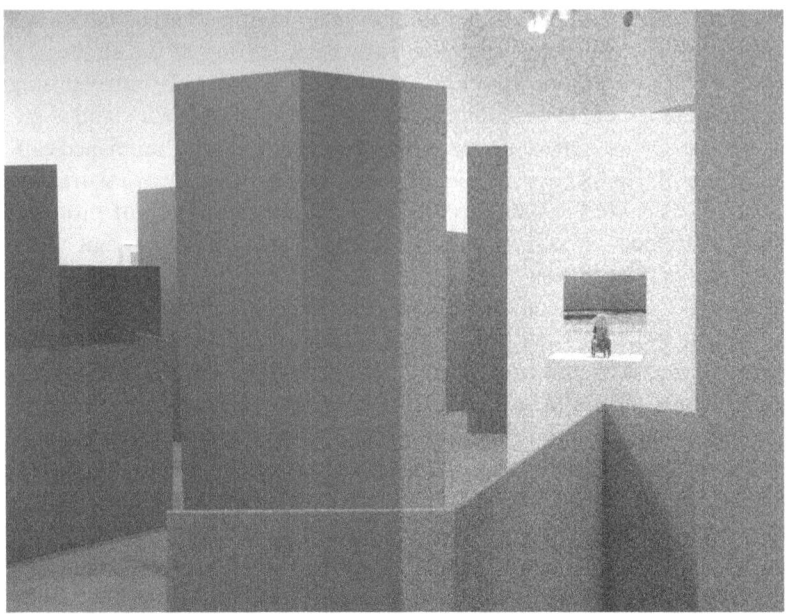

Figure 1.3 Rachel Harrison, *Perth Amboy*, 2001

Installation view, "Consider the Lobster," curated by Tom Eccles, Center for
Curatorial Studies, Bard College, Annandale-on-Hudson, New York, June 27 –
December 20, 2009

Mixed media: twenty-one chromogenic prints, cardboard and straws, and five
sculptures: *Untitled*, 2001 (Wood, polystyrene, cement, acrylic, Formica, plastic
protective film, and ceramic scholar); *Untitled*, 2001 (Wood, GatorBoard, cardboard, Becky Friend of Barbie doll, thumbtacks, and chromogenic print);
Untitled, 2001 (Plaster bust of Marilyn Monroe in cardboard Stor-All Box and
dolly); *Untitled*, 2001 (Wood, enamel, Native American figurine, framed sunset
photograph, easel, and sunglasses); *Untitled*, 2001 (Wood, La Morena salsa can,
and reproduction of *Archduke Leopold Wilhelm in his Picture Gallery* (1651) by
David Teniers the Younger)

Overall dimensions variable

Courtesy of the artist and Greene Naftali, New York. Photo: Jason Mandella

seeking fulfillment. Hints of this are expressed by Marilyn and Becky,
both infirmed on wheels and fixating indefinitely upon "dumb"
abstractions: expanses of brown cardboard and green billboard,
respectively. More whimsical in tone are the dogs, chief, and scholar,
but they may (mis)represent a range of selves—genders, ethnicities,
cultures—and a similar tension derived from wondering what they
might possibly gain from the specific objects that they look upon. It

is just as plausible and valid to say that the objects themselves are merely incidental, and ultimately arbitrary.

However, it is the abrupt ways in which they are experienced and juxtaposed within the gallery which prevent me from ever dismissing these arrangements as one-liners. The display may be appreciated as a brand of absurdity that is potentially profound—and capable of functioning as critique of what it means to look at, to collect, and to arrange things with debatable value. Indeed, closer examination reveals that some pedestals are "adorned" with casually strewn strips of masking tape and partially peeled plastic wrap: Harrison's support surfaces consistently subvert standards of museum-quality design, allowing for more parodic questioning of whether these materials should operate with institutional authority, with a currency and clarity that may be consumed efficiently, perhaps with a straw. Indeed Harrison allows plinths to play crucial compositional roles—as sculptural statements comparable to the hanging walls seen in *Snake in the Grass*—which encourage an ambivalence about whether or not to read them as integral parts of assemblage works, rather than as support surfaces for the "real" art products.

But then I finally take heed of a more tourism-worthy subject on the relatively sturdy, white gallery walls surrounding the maze, lined with photos of a second-floor apartment in the New Jersey town of Perth Amboy, where the Virgin Mary reportedly made an appearance in a window. Aside from a few uninhabited shots of the working-class house, most of these images depict visitors touching the smudged glass. The window became a palimpsest of earnest prayers. Some reach for the window with one hand while holding prayer beads or a child in the other. Others are more assertive in their use of both arms for the gesture. The pilgrims' faces appear hazy within, their anonymity ensured by horizontal bars which might prevent those divinely inspired to make a leap of faith out the window. While surrounded by these images—all depicting gestures of devout belief, and composed with care by Harrison herself—I must consider how they compete with the (mostly) found objects inhabiting the cardboard labyrinth. In some sense, I would suggest that this competition allows abstraction to resonate and play a critical role in our experience, in ways that imply a questioning and skeptical worldview, one concerned with doubting received beliefs and social conditioning about how we should look and learn—when streaks and smudges on a window become the basis for a Christian shrine, when an unusable envelope becomes a monument, when a foam blob becomes a vehicle for Zen-like meditation and enlightenment.[8]

Perth Amboy recalls Dan Graham's *Homes for America* (1966–67). In both works, reductive, repetitive, serial, and minimalist qualities are featured, but opened up to social and satirical contexts, while also blurring the division between sculptural and photographic practice. Tom Eccles has mentioned the relevance of Graham's work, focusing on Harrison's positioning of Becky staring at a photograph of a "blue screen"—taken at Pinewood Studios in London—as contrasting remarkably with the high-production values, digital slickness, and monumentality of Andreas Gursky's photographs, exhibited at the Museum of Modern Art in 2001, the same year that *Perth Amboy* was first shown. Graham's work was originally presented as a slide show, based on photos taken with a Kodak Instamatic on train rides home through suburban tract housing in New Jersey. A later version was a page layout for *Arts Magazine*, but was originally intended for a mainstream periodical (*Esquire*), which included the photos accompanied by short texts. Graham's work should be read as a parody of "feel good" packaged lifestyle articles, the sort that appeared in magazines that promise utopian fulfillment within the scores of new communities sprouting up throughout the country at the time. Of course, Graham's piece is comparable to David Foster Wallace's satirical article "Consider the Lobster." Dan Graham has commented on his satirical intent:

> What people misunderstood was that the work was not an attack on Minimalist art at all … it was basically flat-footed humor, the parody of the think-piece that *Esquire* used to have critiquing the suburbs. If anything, it comes more from "Nowhere Man" by the Beatles and "Mr. Pleasant" by the Kinks.

While Harrison's brand of comedy may initially entertain, it tends to come with costs and complications. The philosopher Agnes Heller portrays some of the greatest subversive works of humor as assemblages, which complexly combine comedic tendencies: satire, irony, grotesquery, parody, caricature.[9] Of particular relevance are existential or "tragicomedies," which stage characters not based, in a detailed way, on historically or socially known individuals; they face conflicts and challenges in stylized ways that signify the marginality or "difference" of the human condition. One trait that commonly contributes to an atmosphere of tragic-comedic difference is a sense of absurd predicament: characters seem destined to pursue goals unsuited to them, and must do so through to the (bitter) end. Such characters may absurdly repeat behaviors and gestures—either spoken or performed physically—which are deemed by the majority to be excessive, unproductive, or otherwise abnormal; such characters may inhabit stories that poke fun, often inadvertently, at sentimental desires for redemption and fulfillment (through, say, spiritual or consumerist means). Narrative incidents are never neatly resolved; paradoxes and ambivalences persist so that "whatever is ridiculed is also mourned; the thing that has been lost is mocked, but the loss still hurts.

An aura of mysticism can surround the absurd drama." For Heller, emotional reaction to tragicomic experience is always mediated by the intellect; so that the immediacy of laughter is tempered by lingering (or loitering) reflection, and eventually may develop into melancholic haze. Indeed, one may at first chuckle when confronting the likes of a Becky or Marilyn, but then there is a need to contend with their predicaments, with their debilitated or marginalized conditions—as well as their behaviors, plights, and compulsions—and their uncertain associations with the maze and with the photos taken in Perth Amboy.

Such complications recur in Harrison's *Indigenous Parts IV* (1995–2009), which features a plethora of pedestals. Perhaps they were found on site, in storage rooms—suitable material for an impromptu arranging activity, resulting in a disorienting structure comparable to the cardboard maze: some plinths are stacked to form a makeshift wall, while others are carved up, overturned, or have their unpainted innards exposed. With rough edges and compromised positions, some are forced to serve dysfunctional roles as shelving systems for things normally encountered in convenience stores, junk shops, and big-box retailers. But some of the configurations are reminiscent of old-school television sets and desktop computers—signs for obsolete screens that once had a three-dimensional presence. And some seem like bolstering devices, just things at hand with mass and weight—temporary backdrops, upon which other things lean provisionally. Finally, some have been sullied with smears of paint—supplying a hint of malicious defacement, mixed with the faint suggestion of gestural expressivity. One pedestal serves as a display stand for a Chevy Impala SS toy model—and an Italian sign for cakes with prices in Euros. A dirty, crumpled potato-chip bag (lightly salted) is stuffed into the base of a yellowish brown sculpture—one with fairly pronounced scatological qualities—perched atop a pedestal with irreverent gray streaks smeared across it. Elsewhere, there is a script from a Surrealist play by Jack Smith, *Brassieres of Atlantis: A Lobster Sunset Pageant*, placed in a steel mixing bowl, as well as a portrait painting featuring a smiling female face being engulfed by swirls of flowers, leaves, and lines. Such is the stage set for Harrison's production, featuring an eccentric cast of cobbled-together (non)characters that somehow manage to morph between multiple identities as consumer products, packaging, kitsch, advertising imagery, and abstract objects of contemplation. Within this conglomeration lies a form of humor that depends on an ironic process of questioning the value and the currency of its "indigenous parts."

Some of these parts are abstract and amorphous sculptures, positioned and combined with the pedestals and other materials so that they suggest personages. A battered stepladder serves as the lower body for a sculpture wearing a plastic pink construction hat. Arch-like and

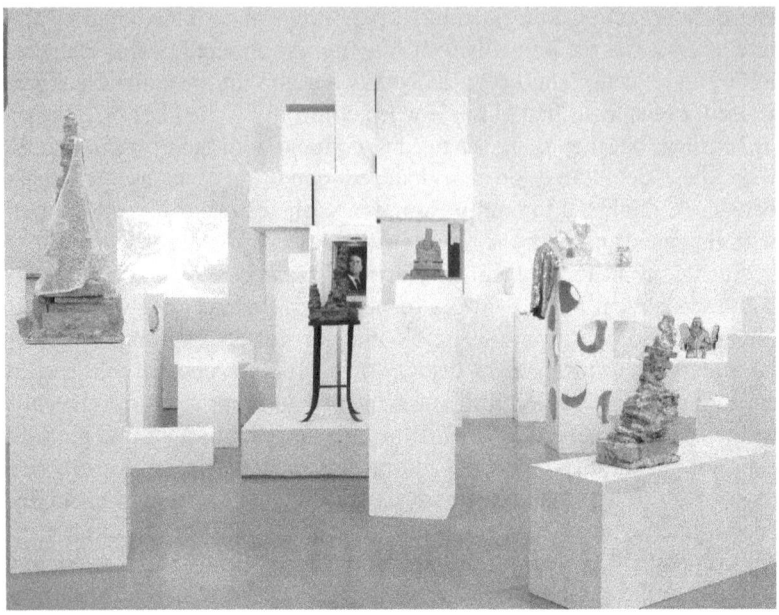

Figure 1.4 Rachel Harrison, *Indigenous Parts IV*, 1995–2009
Installation view, "Consider the Lobster," curated by Tom Eccles, Center for
Curatorial Studies, Bard College, Annandale-on-Hudson, New York, June 27 –
December 20, 2009
Wood; polystyrene; cement; acrylic; knit jersey; dirty lightly salted potato chips
bag; rusty barstool; wooden stepladder; plastic construction hat; sequined skirt;
fabric; mixing bowl; *Brassieres of Atlantis: A Lobster Sunset Pageant* play script
by Jack Smith; painting; cyst tube; set of Modiano Napoletane playing cards;
glass jar; jump ropes; Bar Keepers Friend cleaner; foam art-handling block; ice-
cream sign; Bard College folding chairs; pizza peel; pigmented inkjet prints of
Cher, Mel Gibson, Moses, and Ronald Reagan mounted on foam core; *Ants*,
digital video, color, silent, 29:00 min (1995/2003); *Fleischmanns' Auction*, digital
video, color, silent, 27:44 min (2003); *Buddha*, sculpture (2009); *Telephone
Booth*, sculpture (2009); and *Florida Orange Grove*, chromogenic print (1995)
$180 \times 497 \times 356$ inches ($457.2 \times 1262.4 \times 904.2$ cm)
Courtesy of the artist and Greene Naftali, New York. Photo: Jason Mandella

made up of stacked strata, this body shows signs of deterioration—a bit
like an ancient ruin that is no longer structurally sound—but coated in
a decidedly non-architectural, light pink concoction which matches the
hat. This character combines an indirect reference to the monumental
with male and female qualities (construction and pink), and is reminiscent of gay culture or forms of camp and masquerade that may seem
outdated (Village People). Elsewhere, a tiny sequined skirt hangs from a

bright yellow sculpture, another potentially outdated sign for a sexually "out there" scene (disco); "she" has been placed on the (metaphorical) pedestal, but this platform has been crudely cut up into a Swiss cheese. Another sculpture resembles a stalagmite, a natural accumulation, but has been immersed in synthetic, greyish goo; he or she dons a similarly skimpy, perforated white undershirt, but only on one shoulder, a flirtatious gesture; this flimsy garment may be an allusion to the muscle club scene (Muscle Mary). One wonders whether these figures may be on their way to registering as social types, or if they actually supply sufficient specificity as sociological portraits. Another rock-like protuberance is replete with a repellent stew of rust, pink, and purple. This form sits upon an antique wooden chair, also supporting a photograph of a painting of Ronald Reagan; it seems an unusual portrait, as the sitter looks remarkably disgruntled.[10] Perhaps he is reacting with repulsion to the queer company surrounding him, or to the portraitist's treatment of him—and its subsequent insertion into an assemblage that starkly contrasts, in a satirical way, with the tradition of presidential statuary. Harrison's treatment may take a bite out of its Republican referent, but whatever dissing that is detectable is complicated by its competition with the abstract sculpture and those relatively refined and flared wooden legs (which differ from the beat-up stepladder).[11]

But this Reagan may be read in dialogue with other pictures of prominent Americans included in *Indigenous Parts*: nearby a faded and ghostly reproduction of a 1970s or early 1980s poster of Cher, scantily clad, casually leans on a pedestal. Notable is her status as a queer icon, and one imagines her sliding into the sequined skirt. Hiding elsewhere is a Mel Gibson poster—depicting the actor in the heroic *Braveheart* role of the freedom fighter William Wallace—placed upside down within a hollowed-out pedestal. More prominently placed is a picture portraying another legendary leader, prepared to sacrifice all to liberate his people: Moses is known to many of us in the guise of Charlton Heston—like Reagan, a quintessentially American actor with right-wing beliefs—displayed in luscious big-screen Technicolor. Harrison supplies a crappy found image of Moses carrying the tablets—stone monuments inscribed by God as a vehicle for laying down the law—but here his face is a corpse-like grey-blue, his shaggy beard a pukey green, and his robe is patchwork of clashing colors. Why is Harrison rendering this biblical figure as a pixelated poster, and enlarging from a low-resolution (outdated) source? An endlessly circulated image, he is here rendered as a tangible thing, fastened to a support of cheap foam core. A biblical hero is rendered as an utterly inconsequential doodle, an arbitrarily conjured confection. Through caricature and other means, Harrison serves up characters who have played the role of prophets, fighting for freedom—from enslavement, from oppression, from sexual repression or persecution. How often have we consumed such characters as packaged goods, with unquestioning ease, with full and immediate comprehension? Harrison encourages such questioning by absurdly combining her personages with abstract objects, and imagery drawn from contrasting contexts: high art and lowly kitsch, urban and rural, religious and secular, literary and visual—as well as elements that uneasily occupy in-between zones, shifting back and forth between the rarified and commonplace worlds.[12]

This sort of heterogeneity is further foregrounded in the video *Fleischmanns' Auction* (2003), also included in *Indigenous Parts IV*. The work documents small-town citizens of all ages selling off stuff with little or no worth in the conventional sense: a bad painting, a mask, a pipe cutter, a painted saw—all are included on the same level playing field. Apparently, just about everything may be sold, and anything may be evaluated as potentially a source of value or utility (aesthetic or otherwise).[13] This may be a sociological investigation into a rural community's lifestyle (and frugality).[14] These days, big-city auctions are increasingly structured so that people may participate remotely (via telephone or online), but the Fleischmanns event is strictly hands-on, focused resolutely on what we can see and handle in the flesh (no white gloves required); in contrast to Sotheby's spectacles, Fleischmanns stages its production with no podium or other pretentious props.[15] However, like the artist, they exhibit a form of difference: they are preoccupied with collecting stuff that (privileged) others would normally judge as obsolete, and discard as refuse.[16] Among other things, the work represents such outsiders, in their prolonged circulation and consumption of aged stuff from a consumerist world dominated by the imperatives of newness and novelty. However, this video—in its literal representation of people—is presented within a diverse display of other imagery and objects that are abstract and indirect in their human significations.[17]

Straining our ability to anthropomorphize, Harrison ironically forces objects into playing human roles in obviously inadequate ways, so that they always register, in part, as *only* materials, colors, textures, or reductive and minimal forms; such considerations are permeated by a sense of utter inadequacy, and this sense alternates between tragic and absurd connotations. For Gilles Deleuze, one purpose of humor is to demonstrate that people are the products of a milieu or an "environment of sense" which goes beyond the system of language, into a realm of abstraction associated with nonverbal experience.[18] For Deleuze, "humor beyond irony" is an art of surfaces, or the creative practice of thinking the noises, sensations, and sensible singularities from which bodies are composed. To be humorous, these singularities may be brought into uneasy relationships and multiplicities, but never packaged seamlessly into a coherent set of unities, structured according to a logic of before and after. In this regard, it is helpful to consider Samuel Beckett's plays, as they present characters, sets, and events that are remarkably minimal and inadequate by conventional standards. Exhibiting a radical lack of narrative incident and development, *Endgame* (1957), for instance, features several static characters that are infirmed. Hamm is an aged blind master who cannot stand and his servant Clov cannot sit. Mutually dependent, they have fought for years and continue to do so. Clov always wants to leave but seems unable. Also present are Hamm's legless parents, Nagg and Nell, who live in dustbins upstage; they request food or argue inanely. Repeating dialogue incessantly, Beckett's characters are akin to Harrison's sculptural personages: in their simple immobility, these anti-heroes often seem object-like, with so few attributes or behaviors that the audience may conflate them with the "dumb" material that they are juxtaposed with: dust, sheets, bins, and the like. Similarly, in Beckett's *Play* (1963), a man, his wife, and his mistress stand in identical gray funeral urns; the audience only sees their heads, as they tell three "truths" which appear largely disconnected; despite their love triangle, they seem incapable of coherent communication. When an individual character speaks, his or her predicament is literally highlighted, as a single interrogating spotlight shines on a face, while the others wait in darkness for their turn.[19]

A comparable sense of tragicomedy is relevant, I would argue, to Harrison's personages identified with American nationalism—conventionally staged within museums in a didactic fashion, traditionally as monumental statements designed to impose and impress. As in the case of Reagan, Harrison is of course fond of engaging in a mocking dialogue with genres of portraiture and statuary.[20] *Rainer Werner Fassbinder* (2007) features a female mannequin wearing a t-shirt, leggings, and glasses, with a Dick Cheney mask fastened to the back of her head. The figure offers an empty hand, which in a retail setting might contain a product for sale: within this two-faced context, this registers as a gesture of deception ("What is Dick trying to sell me? Perhaps a war meant to liberate persecuted people in a foreign land?"). The figure leaves a trail of packing peanuts: weathered foam nuggets, perhaps a playful reference to a path of destruction, a wake of wastefulness, the worthless consequence of warmongering ambition. Of course, this work encourages the productive merging of identities: the ex-Vice President is spliced with Fassbinder, a filmmaker with a subversive reputation.[21] Traditionally, satire must take the form of an attack on a specific individual or target. Satire is conventionally defined in terms of an immediate target of attack (a person or social group); the sting of Harrison's satirical strike may be felt in a personal sense (anti-Cheney) but this effect easily slips away, in favor of a more diffused critique.

In my case, Harrison's gesture is experienced as slow-burning irony, rather than as a quick-witted maliciousness (a momentary "diss"). As with Reagan, Harrison employs forms to represent Cheney in a way that ensures a negative portrayal, but the diffusion permits viewers to consider the notions of evil, wrongdoing, or folly in ways that certainly stray from one individual's awful deeds.[22] Within her sprawling exhibition, this work may be read as one in a series of stand-ins for a class of people—often those with power and who make promises, or serve as vehicles for fantasy and projection—that are being critiqued and questioned: however, the mannequin is designed to encourage consumer desire in storefront settings; they act as place holders, rather than as receptacles for definitive, efficiently communicable meanings that are firmly planted in stone (as in the case of a marble presidential monument or library). It is crucial to emphasize that Harrison's scale remains resolutely human; this commitment serves to encourage associations with human consequences.

Harrison's work refers to Dada assemblages featuring mannequins and tailor's dummies, such as George Grosz and John Heartfield's *The Middle-Class Philistine Heartfield Gone Wild (Electro-Mechanical Tatlin Sculpture)* (1920) which combines references to the body with home furnishings as a means to protest the destructive senselessness of warmongering and bourgeois consumerist cultures. Grosz and Heartfield envisioned such works as an ironic critique of the technological and consumerist worlds, referring to themselves as "engineers" and their works as "products." With its lit bulb, this assemblage may function as a lamp, but of course makes reference to the aftermath of war and imperialism, and how the wounded may be enlisted by ideologues as mere props. Like Harrison's work, Grosz and Heartfield's character exhibits gender ambiguity: he/she can be manipulated, with a light that may be turned off and on at will; his/her body is used as a posting place for ornaments.

In the same gallery stands Harrison's *The Eagle Has Landed* (2006), with its titular referencing of war (and a legendary war movie by the same name). It includes an amorphous sculpture, adorned with a sickly concoction of hues, suggesting an unbridled activity of indiscriminate accumulation (or conquest). And yet to my surprise, compared to *Fassbinder*, I empathize with this tangible thing as an unfortunate creature, formerly full of pride; the sympathy derives in part from a sense of the object being handcrafted, rather than simply found and positioned there. And it has been laid to rest, with a patriotic pillowcase depicting an eagle, draped over its "face"—rendered flightless, upended and exhausted upon a mundane table, registering quite unexpectedly as a sign for a regime, or a nation, that has really done wrong. It encourages me to consider the costs of such wrongs

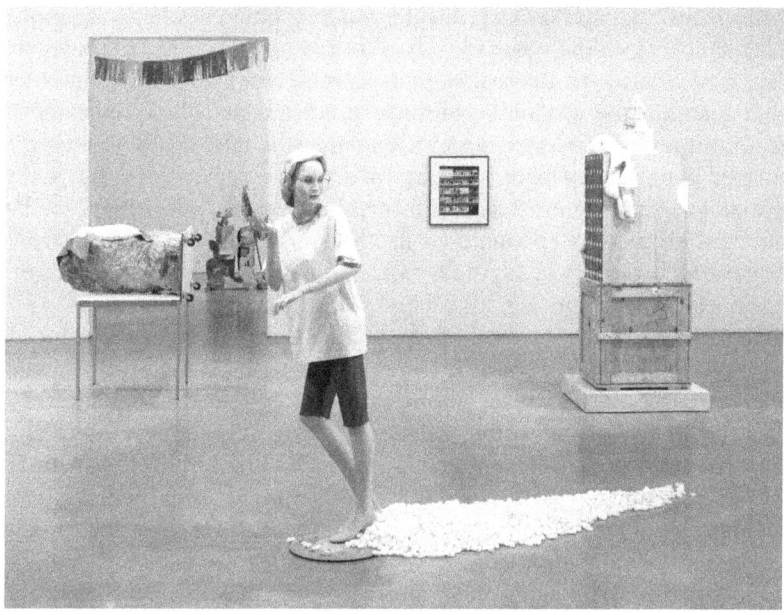

Figure 1.5 Rachel Harrison, *Rainer Werner Fassbinder* (2007)
Installation view, "Consider the Lobster," curated by Tom Eccles, Center for
Curatorial Studies, Bard College, Annandale-on-Hudson, New York, June 27 –
December 20, 2009
Courtesy of the artist and Greene Naftali, New York. Photo: Jason Mandella

and transgressions, committed within other settings as well (like the
banking system).

When experienced in succession within the show at Bard, Harrison's
works became quite productively unhinged from forms of critique
dedicated definitively to any particular historical moment or agent: they
exceed any attempts at reduction to any specific satirical or polemical
argument about, say, imperialism or the greed-soaked, right-wing pursuit of power. And it is these gestures toward abstraction—the unruly
mass beneath the pillow case, the offering of the empty hand, the indiscriminate sprays of color on cubic plinths—that give Harrison's project
its wide-ranging resonance. Literal and abstract elements are slapped
together, thus complicating any single-minded gestures toward characterization and personification. These kinds of juxtaposition encourage
us to actively project, and to consider contexts of politics and consumption in which we are all, in some way, complicit.

Harrison tends to alter consumer products, but only rarely dissolves
or masks them completely. Dousing, sticking, contorting, degrading,

lowering, and battering: the procedures exerted on these materials do subvert, in part, marketing strategies that rely on an aesthetic of immediate enjoyment. She stages displays that exude notions of the fragmentary and abused, to the extent that we must contend with characters that seems to be straining, within a predicament. This predicament is a notion that I am striving to articulate: it is integral to an identity formed in uneasy dialogue with several display contexts simultaneously, a dialogue that therefore resists motives of efficient marketing, packaging, and sale—as encountered in museums, stores, and elsewhere.[23] Harrison's project is, always in a partial sense, resistant to standards of curatorial professionalism associated with the efficient exercise of contextualization and education of the public: it cannot be easily reduced to bullet points in a curatorial argument. This resistance to language fuels a sense of optimism about satirical approaches that uneasily and disjunctively employ characters and motifs that appear partial or limited: with "bodies" that are beat-up plinths or amorphously abstract blobs, undoubtedly unsuitable as spokespeople for a particular political agenda, advertising message, or didactic program. Her juxtaposed characters are anti-protagonists who play their roles badly, with inadequate props and staging, their ironic combination of literal imagery (the image of Mel Gibson, the Dick Cheney mask) and the less articulate material aspects of human experience may express how "the wonder that prompts romantic striving often leads to unintelligible abstraction."[24] Indeed, Harrison's project cannot accommodate heroes in any conventional sense: she presents selves that are always already compromised and complicated.

Notes

1 Curated by Tom Eccles, Harrison's exhibition was held at CCS Hessel Museum, Bard in 2010. My reading addresses a selective portion of this version of the show. The show traveled as "HAYCATION," curated by Daniel Birnbaum and Melanie Ohnemus, Portikus, Frankfurt am Main (2010); and "Conquest of the Useless," curated by Iwona Blazwick, Whitechapel Gallery, London (2010).

2 Actually, it is a former directory from the offices of FEGS (Federation, Employment, and Guidance Service), a non-profit health and human-services organization in New York, funded by the United Jewish Appeal (UJA) Federation. For further discussion of *Snake in the Grass*, see Elisabeth Sussman's review of "Consider the Lobster" in *Artforum* 48, no. 3 (November 2009) and David Joselit, "Touch to Begin," in Eric Banks and Sarah Valdez, eds., *Rachel Harrison: Museum With Walls* (Annandale-on-Hudson, London, and Frankfurt: Center for Curatorial Studies, Bard College; Whitechapel Gallery; and Portikus, 2010), 186–99.

3 The text was originally published in *Gourmet Magazine* (August 2004). It has a remarkable subversive and satirical edge, as it does not focus on food but rather on philosophical, sociological, and scientific questions, such as whether lobsters can feel pain. See Wallace, *Consider the Lobster and Other Essays* (New York: Back Bay Books, 2006), 240, 235–54.

4 For discussion see, for instance, Dustin Griffin, *Satire: A Critical Reintroduction* (Lexington: University Press of Kentucky, 1994), 35–70.

5 Comparing Harrison's compositional strategies with Robert Rauschenberg's Combines, Jack Bankowsky points out how her works situate every-thing—from pure paint to tabloid drivel—so that things never "really come together ... They coexist ..." hence encouraging a thought process that lies relatively close to the edge of meaninglessness. See Bankowsky, "Monkey House Blessing Potpourri," in *Rachel Harrison: Museum With Walls* 136–47. Similarly, David Joselit deals with how Harrison refuses to absorb readymade materials into a composition, but rather "host[s] them in a lim-inal state where association is both promiscuous and obscure." Interestingly, Joselit observes how Harrison renders spectatorship as a form of searching akin to search engines in which "noise" is brought into an uneasy combin-ation with communication: paintings and found things unexpectedly lie in the cavities of pedestals, but never fully or securely inhabit them. See Joselit, "Touch to Begin ..." in *Rachel Harrison: Museum With Walls*, Please see note 2. 192.

6 For a perceptive treatment of the notions of "inadequation" and trans-missibility, see Giorgio Agamben, *The Man Without Content* (1994), trans. Georgia Albert (Stanford, CA: Stanford University Press, 1999), 106–14.

7 For helpful commentary on the idea of obsolescence in Harrison's work, see Johanna Burton, "Just Past: Rachel Harrison's Lagerstätten," *Parkett* 76 (2006): 150–54. Burton points out Harrison's preference for incorpor-ating references, to pop and consumer cultures, that are neither relevant "out there" nor digested enough to fully assume the mantle of high culture "in here"; these images and materials may be pleasing in their own right, but have a stubbornly material presence that is irreducible to "ideas" (154).

8 In addition to the face of the Mary, Perth Amboy pilgrims reportedly also encountered streaks of changing colors—reddish orange, white and brown, grayish green with a touch of red—a multi-hued spectacle analo-gous to Harrison's stack of straws, but relatively abstract, amorphous, and not empirically or visually verifiable, a bit like the Burning Bush (see the *New York Times* article, reproduced in *Museum with Walls*).

9 See, for example, Heller, *Immortal Comedy: The Comic Phenomenon in Art, Literature, and Life* (Oxford: Lexington Books, 2005), 94–124. Thanks to Juliane Rebentisch for pointing me in the direction of Heller's work.

10 The image is actually a quotation from part of an installation by Hans Haacke, *Ölgemälde, Homage a Marcel Broodthaers* (*Painting in Oil, Homage to Marcel Broodthaers*), originally shown at Documenta 7 (1982): Haacke hung a portrait painting of Ronald Reagan (executed by the artist), with its intended implications of stately respectability, opposite a large-scale image

of a crowd protesting in Bonn against Reagan's lobbying for the deployment of American missiles in Germany. In keeping with her more broadly satirical approach, Harrison's fragment omits the protest image and hence avoids the particular political issue addressed by Haacke's work.

11 Relevant in this regard is John Kelsey's thoughtful discussion of how Harrison's installations may distract us from a purely sculptural condition: such works feel more like "complexes" than "combines," in which a paint gesture feels more like a rash or a sort of betrayal. Her figural forms register as "stand-ins or imposters," playing the role of verticality as a kind of camp routine, acting as placeholders against definitive meanings that derive from being firmly planted, like "real" statues. See Kelsey, "Sculpture in an Abandoned Field," in *Rachel Harrison: Voyage of the Beagle* (Zurich: Migros Museum für Gegenwartskunst, 2007), 120–25.

12 As Johanna Burton has pointed out, Harrison's works maintain the importance—or at least the insistence—of everything that seems somehow unfit for exhibition, while also calling attention to the arbitrariness of systems of intellectualized ranking, like those employed in museums. See Burton, "Just Past: Rachel Harrison's Lagerstätten," *Parkett* 76 (2006): 150–54.

13 Also included in the installation is the assemblage *Buddha* (2009), which features a pedestal, painted bright orange, upon which are placed, in an orderly fashion, a smattering of similarly inconsequential things: a fake mango with pins stuck in it (voodoo?); a sharpie pen; a rock; a rolling pin; a miniature set of playing cards; and a Buddha figurine topped with a plastic baguette and a wooden stick. Aside from a pronounced reference to Dali, the work suggests a spiritual, shrine-like context but one complicated by the "worthless" offerings on hand.

14 Projected on a wall in a peripheral part of the installation is the silent video *Ants* (1995/2003), a study of several species' colonies and living habits—perhaps comparable to the documentary premise underlying *Fleischmanns' Auction*, but it is perhaps more relevant to read the imagery as analogous to the colonizing behaviors of capitalist and consumerist cultures.

15 There have been earlier incarnations of *Indigenous Parts* that similarly incorporated the small abstract sculptures: Harrison's emphasis on recycling material corresponds to a refusal to submit to the norm of providing packaged, novel, and spectacular experiences.

16 Fleischmanns is a village located in upstate New York.

17 Beckett's theatre may strike humorous notes when, for instance, the order of time and explanation no longer holds (not because it is meaningless), as in *Endgame* (1957): Question: "What time is it?" Answer: "The same as usual." Unlike Socratic irony—which insists on what concepts must mean—Beckett's humor perverts conceptual meaning, saying what we cannot say. With this form of humor, the self appears less as an organized agent and more as a collection of incongruous body parts. The self is no longer a centralized subject—capable of a distant, synthesizing point of view—but one that is an ad hoc, dynamic, disconnected, and disrupted series of connections. This species of humor takes the self "down" to its corporeal origins, unlike conventional kinds of irony, which strive to think the power of subjectivity and synthesis beyond or "above" any of

its specific terms. Deleuze's notion of humor, indeed, is defined in opposition to irony's traditional association with a point of view above existence. His approach spurs us to consider how and why such high–low or before–after distinctions and hierarchies have enabled us to think. It does so by addressing the play of surfaces and doubles, "of nomad singularities and of the always displaced aleatory point ..." See Deleuze, *The Logic of Sense* (1969), trans. M. Lester (New York: Columbia University Press, 1990), 154.

18 See Deleuze, *The Logic of Sense*, 7, 135–38, 141.

19 In *Happy Days* (1961), Beckett empties the stage, save for two characters. Winnie is covered in mold, as she talks to Willie, who is unseen and reading the sports pages. The "plot" here is driven by Winnie's preoccupations— looking in the mirror, putting on makeup, examining a toothbrush or glasses—and fruitless attempts at establishing contact: small talk is mixed with nonsensical chatter or noise. The character's monotonous repetition of dialogue reflects a hunger for communication, which is finally met with a ridiculous pseudo-response by Willie (he eventually says "Win").

20 For discussion of Harrison's work in relation to traditions of statuary, see Richard Hawkins, "Enigmarelle: The Statuesque," *Parkett* 82 (2008): 120– 29, which includes treatment of Dada precedents including Kurt Schwitters's *Second Merz Column* (1923). Schwitters's unmonumental memorial featured a conglomeration of literal and abstract motifs—as well as tragic and comic references—including a weathered pedestal, plastered with print material, and topped with the death mask of his infant son.

21 Ellen Seifermann has observed how Harrison employs names (as in the case of *Cindy* of 2004) so that they become unhinged in relation to their surroundings, akin to the concrete objects that also make up an assemblage, promoting further (and wider) identity speculation among viewers. See Seifermann, "Many Layered Objects: Notes on Rachel Harrison's Strategies," in *Rachel Harrison: Voyage of the Beagle* (Zurich: Migros Museum für Gegenwartskunst, 2007), 116–18.

22 For excellent discussion, see Charles A. Knight, *The Literature of Satire* (New York: Cambridge University Press, 2004), 3–13.

23 For commentary on Harrison's subversive relation to design-and-display cultures—which conventionally succeed in dissolving frontier zones between products and their packaging or presentation—see John Kelsey, "Sculpture in an Abandoned Field," in *Rachel Harrison: Voyage of the Beagle*, 123.

24 For some relevant discussion, see Claire Colebrooke, *Irony* (London: Routledge, 2004).

2 Isa Genzken
"OIL"

Oil is a slippery subject. Prone to processing and myriad forms of manipulation, the substance is shady and seductive, always shifting: from flowing crude to viscous bitumen to solid asphalt.[1] And it is equally susceptible to semantic shifts: prized and vilified, it is as essential to the venerable combustion engine as it is to much future industrial innovation. It is associated with the exploration of frontier landscapes, with the harsh realities of toxic ooze and even with science-fictional sources of sentient life.[2] But as an adjective, the term applies as readily to people as it does to products, plastics, and pigments. Oily people may seem playful, but the purpose of such performing is to persuade—to lay on the charm, while convincing or converting others to believe or behave in ways running counter to their habits, or perhaps their decency. Oil is in just about everything and, by extension, everyone. And so I find that it is an ideal idea to set the metaphorical stage for reading "OIL," Isa Genzken's large-scale installation at the 2007 Venice Biennale—a show largely made up of oil-infused, mundane materials that quite unexpectedly manage to acquire an agency of their own—and a certain kind of urgency, about broken promises and dreams, sold by oily people and associated with oily consumer "goods."

Slippages—between objects and subjects, between products and people—are crucial to my reading of Genzken's project. I would argue that "oil" here might be envisioned as a plague, a form of affliction which, at times, is wrapped up within a staged propaganda production with the labels "liberation" and "progress." It is the sort of message conveyed by individuals and imperialist regimes—from Goebbels to George Bush—but it is always also associated and synonymous with the latest technologies, from military hardware to consumer items that will serve as redemptive rewards for those on the receiving end of liberation.[3] While securing scarce resources and improving their own security, the oily perpetrators package their persecutions with larger-than-life narratives, with glorified monuments, with heroic characters. Such stories are seamlessly orchestrated to impose and impress, to function like a well-oiled machine. In a metaphorically indirect and absurdist manner, Genzken exposes the workings of the machine. Employing run-of-the-mill materials on a down-to-earth scale, she does so by staging characters and scenarios that are anything but glorious. Her non-heroes and anti-monuments seem so tragically and comically inadequate in their roles, compared to those that are so masterfully marketed and designed as nation liberators and the deliverers of progress—so efficiently fed to audiences these days as an enthralling experience, with the aid of infotainment-style factoids, and bathed in bewitching graphics, either online or on Fox News.

Genzken serves up fragmented conglomerations of objects and imagery that are struggling to supply a story. Instead of promises of prosperity and respect for individual rights and freedoms, I encountered assemblages of "selves" that are tainted and tired, repetitive and reductive, belittled and broadsided, compromised and constrained.[4] They are in a predicament, with no hope of functioning efficiently as monuments made to dazzle. Seemingly on the verge of collapsing into mere masses of messy materials, Genzken situates unstable and uneasy unions of sensations and surfaces, bodies and emotions, as well as abstract qualities and gestures that have agencies of their own, from shiny metallic foil to deflated mannequins, from adulterated dolls to crumpled posters of cats.

The German pavilion at the Venice Biennale is a building with baggage—and Genzken expresses this notion literally, and with a subversive relish, as we shall see. But before entering the building, however, it is helpful to briefly consider its circumstances: originally designed by Daniele Donghi, an architect of the Venice City Council, it was largely rebuilt in 1938 by Ernst Haiger, under Hitler's orders. Delicate Ionic columns were replaced by heavy and square Teutonic pillars. A stonemason engraved the word "GERMANIA" on the façade. Parquet flooring was removed in favor of a finely-pored marble, intended to lend an air of chilly consecration. Arno Breker's sculptures, including the heavily muscled statue *Readiness*, occupied the interior.[5] This massive monument was, of course, meant to intimidate visitors, while conveying a message of racial and cultural superiority, associated with muscular bodies and the greatness of ancient empires.[6] Facing the dilemma of what to do with the pavilion, Genzken chooses to cover the fascist façade with scaffolding and an orange mesh curtain—the sort widely used on Italian construction sites—leaving only the entranceway bare.[7] This bright covering is evenly and cleanly distributed, operating as a grid; with no other signs of renovation activity, this intervention seems like a gesture of suppression, intended not as a way of dismissing the building's baggage, but a means of leveling the playing field, allowing visitors to become oily, to slip and slide between contexts: accordingly,

I consider the notions and processes of veiling and draping in them-selves, expressed here on a grand scale, with an all-over uniformity. And so, it is suitable to stray from the specific cases of Germany and the Third Reich—with its monstrous and mammoth characters—specu-lating about the concept of packaging and marketing nations, in sunny shades of orange, or in the form of pavilions, and otherwise.[8] The use of a flexible grid of plastic—a petroleum-based product—triggers a thought about the Biennale's past, as a staging ground, since 1895, for cultural competitions that metaphorically mirror other contests, about the continued conquest of "backward" parts of the world, and the "cul-tivation" of their inhabitants.

Oil: this three-character, single-syllable, tiny term does indeed refer to a host of friendly phenomena—from cuisine to suntans—but just a cursory glance at Genzken's show suggests a context of con-flict, and with the beliefs and desires that are so often linked to oil—including imperialism, cultural superiority, and greed—yet veiled by the premise of setting people free. Snake oil, as it were. In Genzken's show, these ideological qualities operate in relation to multiple and expansive contexts—German and American, recent and historical—including those connected to recent conflicts in oil-rich regions, like the Persian Gulf.

Proceeding inside, I confront consumer goods and odd artifacts arranged in clusters and rows, but in ways which stubbornly resist design cultures wedded seamlessly to strategies of monumental scale and playful immediacy. Genzken offers a procession of assemblages led by a red bag, weathered and unadorned except for a price tag, sig-naling the ideas of processing and circulation—of objects and subjects, commodities and people; relatively bare and vulnerable, this Samsonite has suffered wear and tear: weathered strips of red tape help to ensure its closure, and this encourages my curiosity about unknown—perhaps threatening or incriminating—contents, subject to scrutiny by security officials, who surely would inspect such an object if it were hauled about the gallery by a visitor, a potential perpetrator. Nearby stand some unused bags, vertically stacked and perched on wheels—suggesting the ephemeral nature of these columnar anti-monuments, in contrast to the neo-classical permanency of the pavilion. Posters of canonical paintings are combined with images of dogs and cats, all propped up against, or draped over, these teetering display backdrops. A depiction of a Dachshund, of German ancestry of course, shares one of these portable display spaces with a Rembrandt self-portrait and a Canaletto Venetian canal scene. Another suitcase "wore" a jacket with a stylized bat face—surely a marketable motif, an animal that few of us encounter except in fictionalized forms, as consumable products on movie screens, and in stores. Some bags have their main compartments partially

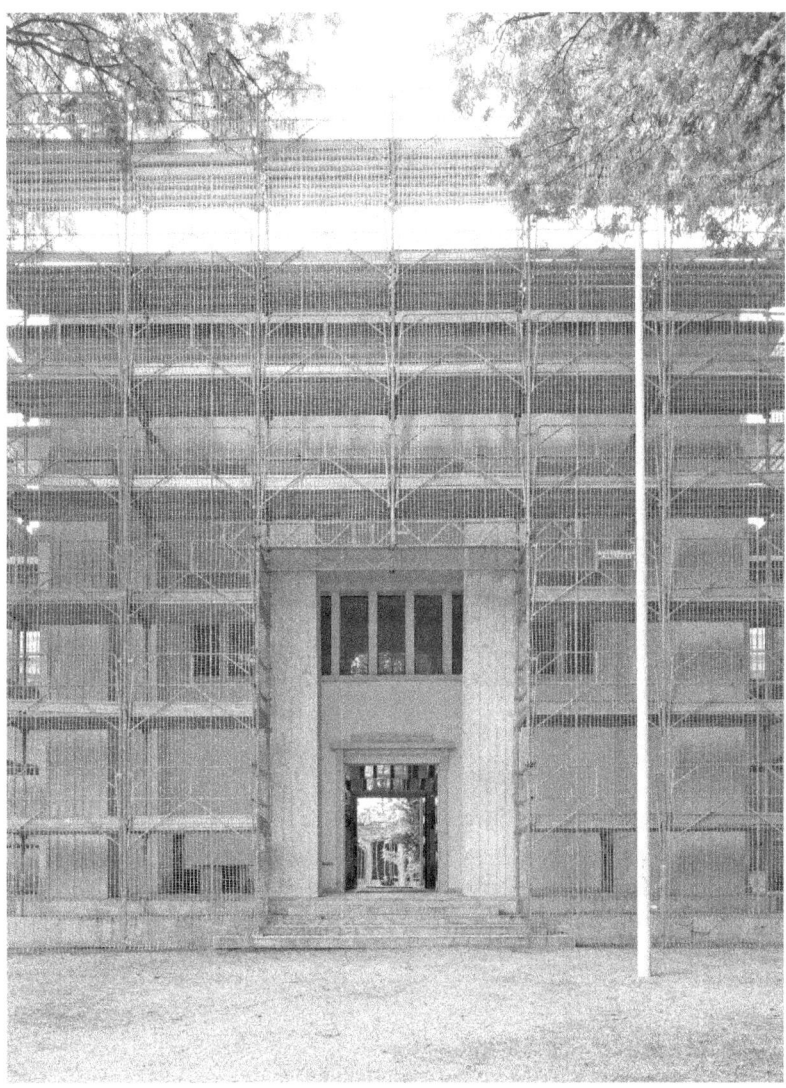

Figure 2.1 Isa Genzken, "OIL," 2007
Installation view German Pavilion, 52nd Venice Biennale 2007
Photo: Jan Bitter. Courtesy of Galerie Buchholz, Berlin/Cologne/New York

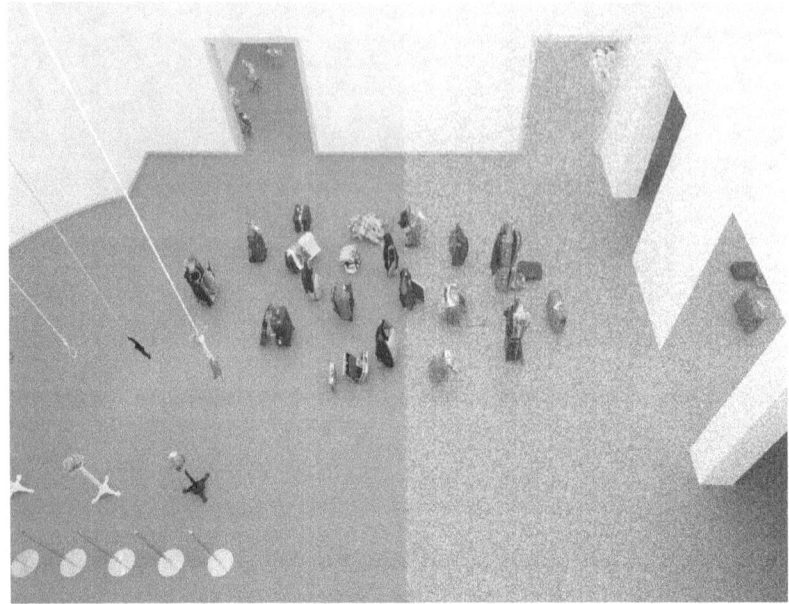

Figure 2.2 Isa Genzken, "OIL," 2007
Installation view German Pavilion, 52nd Venice Biennale 2007
Photo: Jan Bitter. Courtesy of Galerie Buchholz, Berlin/Cologne/New York

unzipped, seductively offering darkened interiors that invite prying
eyes. Indeed, handled recently by most exhibition visitors, luggage is an
item that is especially ripe for uncanny responses, as it is not weighed
down by iconographic traditions. These makeshift pedestals somehow
acquire a sense of agency, as receptacles, providers, and containers of
"content" that are also hollow, precariously positioned. But the cheap
paper products they peddle are accompanied (or hunted) by a group
of predatory birds: perched atop some of these makeshift pedestals are
taxidermied owls—with plumage of brown, white, and gray—a symbol
for flight and the immaterial soul, or for Minerva presiding over the
show, seeking prey in the form of rodents, kitschy imagery, or tourists.
    And yet crucially, these bags have served as support surfaces for
abstract painting as well. These conglomerations of mint-condition
bags, animal corpses, and pictures have been subjected to drizzling—
gestures that initially come across as an act of sullying or tainting—
especially when wedded to such lowly goods, literally built for
abuse: luggage is relentlessly tossed about, thrown on conveyer belts,
prodded into overhead bins. At the end of the luggage procession, a

pair of mirrors hangs on the wall—a diptych which suddenly spurs me into further moments of self-reflection and bodily self-consciousness. While surveying Genzken's extensive painterly additions to her work, I recall *Madonna of the Shadows*, Fra Angelico's fresco (ca. 1440–50) in Florence, where, upon a sizeable section of wall, the artist cast from a distance a rain of colored spots, providing a counterpoint of gesturality and dissemblance to the skillfully imitated faces of a *Sacra Conversazione* scene. For Georges Didi-Huberman, the artist here fulfilled a double requirement—to make present (*à présentifier*) as much as to represent— of offering an abstract expanse of material that is rich in exegetical and contemplative potential, but also a reminder of the humility tied to the pigment-vestiges of the object.[9] Such a spraying activity may reflect a desire for humiliation, expressed during the dissemination of a "pure" material event. It is worthwhile to consider Genzken's activity as a ges- ture of unction, an anointing rite. To anoint is to cast a liquid (oil, tears, paint) onto something or someone that one wants to sanctify, or, more generally, whose symbolic status one wants to modify—as in the case of baptism, sending the dead off to heaven, or the consecration of altars. And this flexibility between people and things, subjects and objects, is relevant to Genzken's practice—as she abstractly anoints a wide range of materials in her exhibition, in a manner that acquires a transgressive charge, given its resemblance to artistic traditions that combine literal imagery with the material and the gestural in themselves, as outlets to express beliefs that cannot be summed up neatly in terms of doctrine— religious, political, or otherwise.

And yet the gesture of throwing liquid paint may also be read as one of trashing—again, this may apply to an idea, person, or thing— associated with cultures of camp, parody, and satire. This gesture may be distinguished from relatively destructive vandalism or outright destruction of an image. In this transgressive context, there is a cru- cial assemblage precedent: the Combines by Robert Rauschenberg that supply the modern (and secular) incarnation of this rite, meant in part as an ironic and mocking critique of Abstract Expressionist ges- tural painting, but also intended as a provocative foray into seemingly uncharted semantic territory, with minimal iconographic baggage. In *Monogram* (1955–59), for instance, no one had yet seen an angora goat wreathed with a tire before—two objects with such strong and separate conventional meanings and material effects, identified with wool and rubber, with sweaters and motor vehicles, respectively. Nor had any- body in a gallery gazed upon drips and slathers of red, white, and green pigment, placed on a stuffed animal's snout. And yet along with the sense of outrageous absurdity, there is a tragic feeling associated with a creature being punished publically, on display in the stocks, as it were. The goat stands upon a square platform "painting"—rather than the respectable standard pedestal he had previously considered using—mounted on coasters, and covered with collage elements, including a child's footprint and a newspaper photo of a parachutist.[10] In his discussion of Rauschenberg's Combine *Bed* (1955) as an "obliquely figurative assemblage," James Leggio considers a range of sacred and profane associations, with the textile components registering as a sincere reference to the bloodstained Shroud of Turin—and yet scribbles, scrawls, and stains contribute to a sense of soiling, sexuality, smearing, and defacement. *Bed* conforms to the proportions of an imagined body that rested on it; the pillow seems a surrogate head, surmounting a kind of schematic torso, implying that the body is pinned or hung from the supporting wall. It is "uncomfortably suspended, streaked with dramatic rivulets of paint running down, it sags like the head of a crucified Christ."[11]

But compared to Rauschenberg's Combines, Genzken's sprawling installation more readily plays a consumerist role. It registers as a display of luggage, providing a selection of product options, with differing attributes and levels of luxury: there are cheaper bags with soft shells, upscale and silvery steel briefcases, and bright-hued, hard-plastic carry-ons. But nearby there is a long row of nooses extending from the ceiling; this is another accumulated catalogue that reflects a consumerist process of selection—offering an array of colors, materials, and thicknesses which serve as a cross-section of a commodity: rope. But attached to these morbid bits of cord are toy monkeys, also varying in type. A diminutive demon is present too. They simply hang about, perhaps oblivious to the usual use-value of nooses. In addition there are two bare nooses, opening up a potential for participation, perhaps by strung-out art tourists. Indeed much of the show served as an ambivalent site for play, with just a whiff of consumer desire, tinged with undercurrents of death. This ambivalence is further complicated by a needling sense of the arbitrary, associated with the idea of *only* arranging objects, like toys and bits of rope, as a display akin to those in shop windows, rather than crafted works worthy of aesthetic contemplation in the conventional sense. As such, when juxtaposed, these objects—monkey and noose—allude to the carefree games of children (who may be oblivious to the deathly subject matter), the non-activity of just clinging to something (or hanging on for dear life), the violence of executioners and persecutors (or the idleness of those whose supposed duty is to capture and punish the unlawful). Genzken's ambivalent brand of humor is expressed in terms of unresolved oppositions, combinations of seemingly unlike elements that are experienced over time. As Gregory Williams has discussed, during the 1980s, Genzken and other German artists of her generation explored mixtures of parodic, satirical, and ironic modes of presentation as means of treating political and topical subject matter "without losing sight of the perceived impossibility of direct action," hence allowing for the Beckett-like possibility of mis-communication and comic failure. Compared to traditional forms of satire—which leave no room for doubt that an object of attack is mor-ally corrupt or socially inferior—Genzken has engaged in forms of parody mixed with irony that can "engage in a critical response without entirely cutting off the possibility for a degree of complicity with its target."[12]

Complicating matters further are faceless mannequins in NASA astronaut suits, suspended from the ceiling. Perhaps kidnapped from some space museum exhibit, here they readily register as instruments of a Cold-War ideological push toward the conquest of lunar surfaces, rather than oil-rich territory. They float euphorically in orbit, perhaps spacewalking and observing an alien (art) world below. They might drift downwards, choosing to end their lives with the nooses at hand, if their mission fails. One dons a helmet with a darkened visor. Defying the laws of gravity—and perhaps other rules too—in their pursuit of space-race victory, they help to signify a broader context of competi-tion that includes the scramble to secure oil supplies. Oily-black posters, with the letters "XXL," stand out as a few of the only pictures actu-ally affixed to walls; indeed, attached to one is the miniscule picture of an astronaut. Genzken's dispersal of retail, museum, and historical reference points suggest, in powerfully allegorical ways, the sprawling scale of capitalist ambition—extra, extra, large, as it were—and the sheer accumulated intensity and immensity of imperialist hunger for territory and resources: black gold and outer space. However, those responsible—legislators and corporate leaders—may envision such activity from a comfortable distance, in aesthetic terms or as simply a game, an amusement that is dressed up or draped in the garb of glory or freedom fighting.

Genzken provides a stage for outsized American ambition and arro-gance, but one that encourages a certain kind of wide-ranging concep-tual and intuitive speculation—stubbornly resistant to being confined along national or historical lines. As before, worth contemplating in this regard is the concept of cultivating unquestioning faith in technological progress, and how that belief is tied to product innovation, heroic per-sonalities, and monumental machines—such as suitably awe-inspiring spacecraft and astronauts, capable of capturing the imagination when served up, seductively and seamlessly, by media providers on flat viewing screens, accompanied by ads. These entertainments are indeed worlds away from Genzken's human-scaled and non-heroic cast of characters, so sculpturally stated.[13] Indeed, her utterly material display comes across as mundane and messy matter, but it compels one to consider how the spectacles of exploration—of new frontiers, of the limits of perceptual

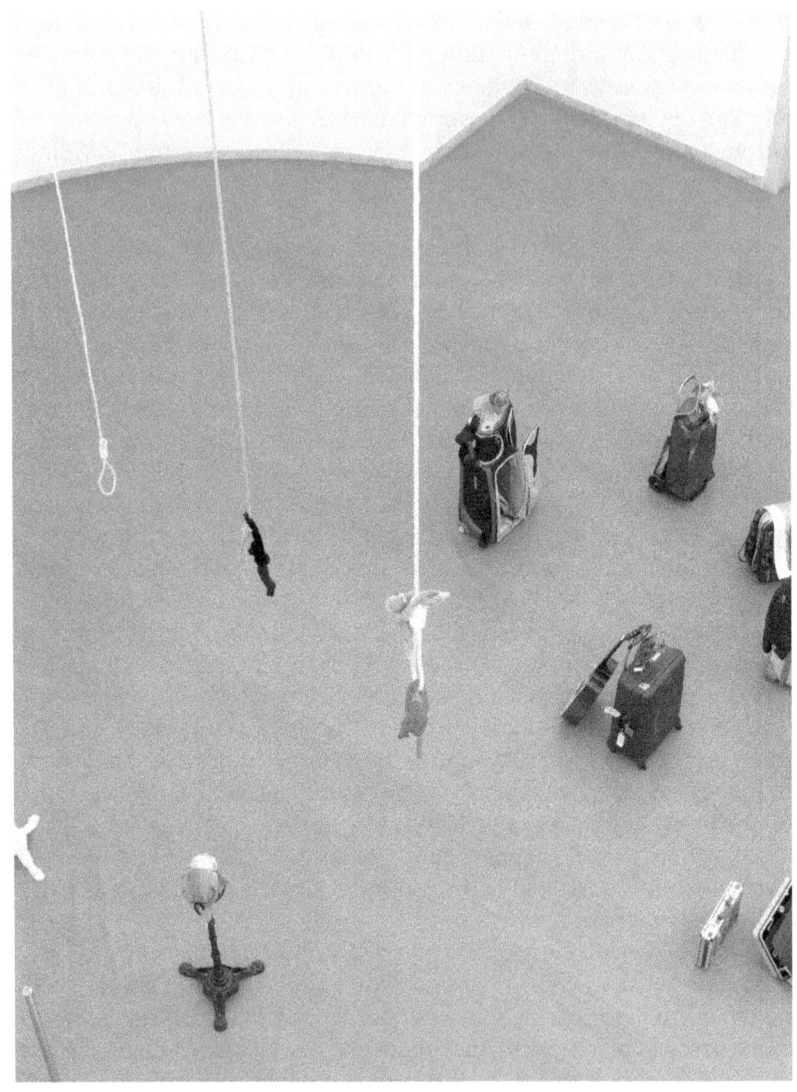

Figure 2.3 Isa Genzken, "OIL," 2007
Installation view German Pavilion, 52nd Venice Biennale 2007
Photo: Jan Bitter. Courtesy of Galerie Buchholz, Berlin/Cologne/New York

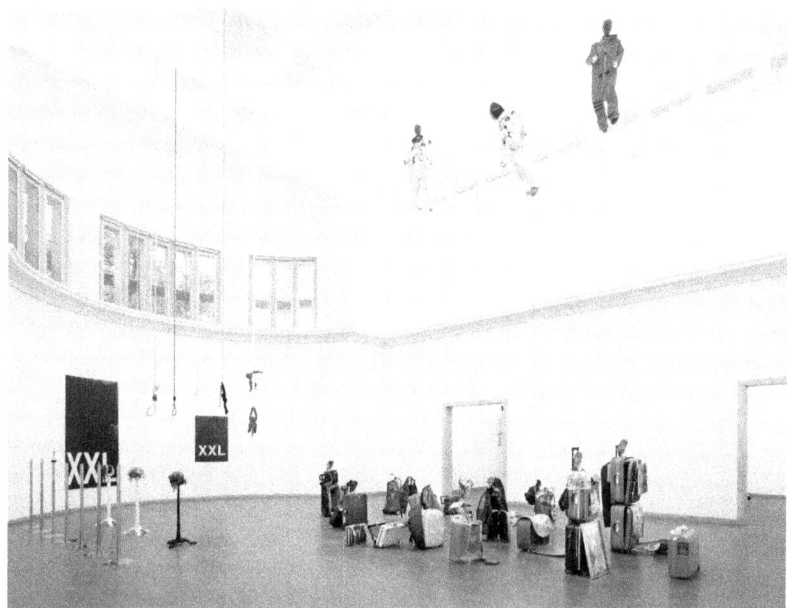

Figure 2.4 Isa Genzken, "OIL," 2007
Installation view German Pavilion, 52nd Venice Biennale 2007
Photo: Jan Bitter. Courtesy of Galerie Buchholz, Berlin/Cologne/New York

experience, of shiny and novel contraptions, of exotic settings—serve as
(oily) deceptions and distractions from the imperatives of conquest and
the coercive conversion to capitalist culture.[14]

Despite its everyday elements and relatively down-to-earth presence,
Genzken's project has a pronounced theatrical nature. Cultures combining masquerade and menace are conveyed by skulls wearing ornate
carnival masks, placed on pedestals in an orderly row. Genzken makes
use of masks that refer to a host of festive spectacles, including Venetian
carnival, which encourage concealment, deception, and excess. These
amusements are fueled by a temporary license to rule-break and
misbehave—transgressive practices that are followed by a sobering
period associated with ritual forgiveness and masquerade removal.
But the artist has combined the masks with skulls, spattered with silver
paint and other adornments—like red teeth and fake eyeballs—that
suggest an activity of vandalizing or defacing. I read these life-sized
heads as all that remains, or as signs of ruin, after an endless cycle of
defying decency, without regard for dire or deathly consequences. What
is left here has no body, and still retains a sense of mocking caricature,

combined with a lingering feeling of monstrous threat. Genzken's gauntlet of disguised characters can take abuse, and yet go on insulting the system, operating with impunity, apparently immune to oversight and censure by governing bodies, like the UN or regulators policing the financial industry.

Contemplation of such offenses, and their dehumanizing consequences, is further encouraged by a series of skull and skeleton ivory figurines, all posing pensively. Placed individually upon metal poles, these creatures invite me to get up close and personal to peruse their particulars, perched on their respective roosts. One character holds a fan while sitting cross-legged, while another rests upon his or her decapitated head. Another brandishes a walking stick, leisurely leaning against a kneeling and praying companion, while another stands next to a jawless skull with a gaping hole, perhaps a sign of divine retribution.[15] The viewer may take heed of them as reminders for the eternal suffering in store for those mask-wearers committing wrongs. Hence these *objets d'art* signal a *memento mori* sentiment—a feeling diffusely present throughout Genzken's installation—which participates in an educational ethos: we must reap what we sinfully sow. But the artist stages this moral message in complicated and compromising ways: the miniatures are placed atop makeshift plinths—slender poles, like those used for crowd control, to keep the little people at bay, which contrast starkly with the pavilion's colossal columns and pilasters, designed to make the public feel insignificant. This juxtaposition—poles and figurines—combines with other assemblage elements to provoke me into an ambivalent mode of viewing which questions the sincerity and seriousness of any message that one may detect. There is the nagging sense that she may only be providing incidental props, never the main event, partly because her display is always associated with a commonplace context that has no gravitas: consumerist browsing and pedestrianism. As mobile agents, visitors must negotiate the poles and contend with subtle product differences, whether it is masks, ropes, or ivories. Indeed, Genzken's work both refers to and resists the tried-and-true pretensions and historical weight of still-life iconography—with its longstanding traditions—in both its pictorial or sculptural incarnations. And she often adopts a minimal logic of seriality, offering repetitive displays that feature reductive and geometric formal vocabularies—which of course fall short when compared to the novelty, scale, and slickness required for the seamless delivery of either serious monuments or blockbuster entertainments. But she lends a sense of humor and a personal touch to such standardized and reductive formats, by personally and manually manipulating much of the imagery and objects on hand. It is these aspects—absurd inadequacies, formal limitations, and playful redundancies—which Genzken uneasily juxtaposes with the dead-serious and the morbid, mixing them into a potent cocktail that is uniquely capable of provoking insights about the destructive costs and ridiculous consequences of being treated inhumanely, and of being instrumentalized repeatedly over time. "OIL" is a site of travesty, a place in which I can taste the palpable flavor of debasement, of what we have become: a grossly inferior imitation of our former selves, creatures that are grotesquely incongruous in style, treatment, and subject.[16]

It is indeed possible to empathize with Genzken's rows of modified poles and suitcases. They are analogous to bodies. With their reductive lines and rectangles composed of shiny plastics and metals, I read them as down-to-earth descendants of human-scaled minimalist cubes from the 1960s, which Michael Fried famously criticized for their anthropomorphism. Fried's annoyance stemmed from minimal objects' unruly, and supposedly troubling, relationship to "other persons": despite their abstraction and thingness, we ascribe or attribute human attributes— converting them into quasi-subjects with a potential volition.[17] As Isabelle Graw has discussed, it is the beholder who must actively speculate about how agency may be assigned to these things, an activity that reflects a culture of questioning the authority of authors similarly rooted in the 1960s.[18] Genzken is in dialogue with inheritors of minimalism who strayed from its relatively rarified aesthetic into the realms of social behaviors, parodic humor, consumerism, and compulsive urges, as in the case of Janine Antoni's *Gnaw* (1992), Dan Graham's *Homes for America* (1966–67), or Mike Kelly's *Lumpenprole* (1991). Genzken does so by combining reductive forms with human figures, including dolls and mannequins placed in laconic, absurd, and grotesque scenarios. Like Graw, I prefer to read such figures metaphorically as the (in)human result of capitalism's more recent incarnations, as a fabrication of our increasingly commodified selves, generating a "massive integration of our personality, our affects, our social relations, and other non-economical aspects of our individual lives."

Another grotesque and serial display is on hand in an adjacent gallery: dolls are placed on chairs and portable stools, all subjected to compromising contortions and other indignities. A formerly green figure, now mostly slathered in silver, wears headphones and does an impossible back bend, enacting a scene of death and play, starring someone with a shattered spinal cord. Wearing a hood and sunglasses, another has a silver skull for a head, and yet is romantically inclined: he or she holds a plastic-wrapped and withered rose bouquet. A "Chucky" figure, with red hair and stains on his face, seems true to character: inverted, yet wielding two knives, ready to wreak havoc.[19] Also present is a gorilla doll engaged in a staring contest with an Elvis action figure who is apparently serenading his simian friend, microphone in hand. And a stool with a pink seat serves as pedestal for a crimson-hued devil, complete with angrily clenched fist. Hovering above, however, is another assemblage—attached with a bracket to the wall—that similarly combines a figure, seating, and painted adornment: occupying a retro 1960s lounger, an earmuff-wearing dummy imbibes something through a long red straw; this infirmed chap is covered crudely with white and silver pigment. Nearby, gleaming metal chairs contain a couple with concerns: an inflatable female (sex) doll lies deflated and limp, with the added adornments of earrings, sunglasses, and a bright red mani-pedi. A metal tube has been inserted in her mouth, and her body and blond tresses are sullied with silver as well. Her companion may have been decapitated, covered (or preserved) in foil, and wrapped in a jacket with orange mesh lining exposed at the cuff. On the floor near them is a half-filled glass, perhaps containing a poison that led to their demises.

Nearby are the "Young Astronauts," two life-sized figures, male and female, lying directly on the floor, with space helmets and high-end sunglasses. One is a dummy similarly covered in silver foil, perhaps a sign for an ongoing mummification or rescue operation—as a shiny provider of warmth by emergency personnel—and therefore a signifier of both preservation. With black hair, blue eyes, and a flowing and elegant dress, his female companion is also deflated and has a pipe in the mouth—and is hence being force-fed, or forcibly kept alive.[20] These comatose anti-heroes—the "Young Astronauts" as a little metal plaque on the wall states—are accompanied by orange plastic containers, perhaps containing organs on ice, or the devices used to revive (or incapacitate) them. All of these figures exude a sense of being on life support, of debilitation combined with notes of perversion, sickness, and monstrosity, made all-the-more poignant when presented on a human scale, and in ways that reference retail, design, and museum display conventions simultaneously. The range of furniture and children's toys on hand never exudes a sense of relaxation or leisure; they are necessary as a comfortable and familiar starting point from which to stray into an uncanny territory of travesty, with the help of additions like the (adult) sex toys and crass paint application: the objects serve as props for a production about both the playing of games and exploitive abuse (sexual, psychological, physical, or capitalist)—and the human costs of conquest.

Genzken's use of modified dummies and dolls is firmly rooted in Dada and Surrealist soil.[21] John Heartfield and Rudolf Schlichter's *Preussischer Erzengel* (*Prussian Archangel*, 1920), for instance, incorporated a papier-mâché pig's head placed atop a body with a WWI German officer's grey garb and accessories; it hung from the ceiling like Genzken's NASA-uniformed figures. This swine-headed puppet was whimsically wrapped with a poster that read "I come from Heaven, from Heaven on high," deriving from a well-known German

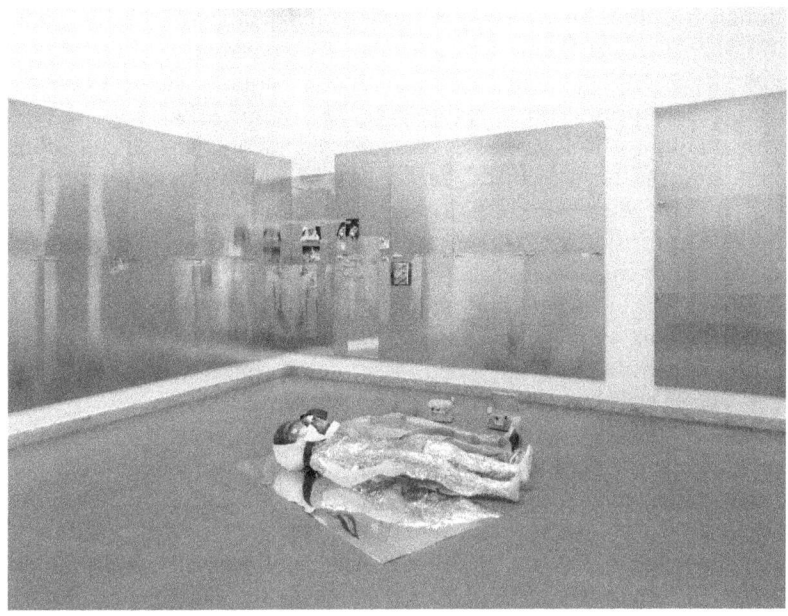

Figure 2.5 Isa Genzken, "OIL," 2007
Installation view German Pavilion, 52nd Venice Biennale 2007
Photo: Jan Bitter. Courtesy of Galerie Buchholz, Berlin/Cologne/New York

Christmas carol, while a sign dangling below further mocked the military: "In order to understand this work of art completely, one should
drill daily for twelve hours with a heavily packed knapsack in full
marching order in the Tempelhof Field [a military training ground in
Berlin]."[22] Genzken's strategy is relatively unhinged and abstracted,
compared to the specific satirical objects of attack preferred by Dada
artists, including the German military establishment. Indeed, hers is
a more dispersed form of critique, with a correspondingly wide range
of historical reference points, including large-scale surrealist projects
incorporating dolls and figures in settings that uneasily combined
retail and museum display qualities. In particular, the 1938 *Exposition
international du surréalisme* in Paris featured female mannequins lined
up in a long, narrow room, greeting visitors.[23] These figures exhibited
signs of abuse and humiliation: Jean Arp's mannequin was covered
with a plastic bag, while André Masson's had her head in a birdcage,
while her mouth was gagged with a velvet band and adorned with a
pansy. Objects were modified in ways that elicited anthropomorphic
reactions of sympathy and morbidity, such as Maurice Henry's

Homage to Paganini (1936/1968), a bandaged violin placed within a miniature coffin, lined with green grass. Genzken's work recalls Dada and Surrealist penchants for subverting conventional notions of creative skill, preferring to arrange and modify "objects" rather than creating "sculptures," transforming everyday things in ways associated with mental pathologies and obsessive behaviors. Surrealists often opted for the term "object" rather than "sculpture" to discourage associations with traditional aesthetics. It is notable that Méret Oppenheim and other female surrealists were not encouraged to take up painting, and so frequently turned to making objects instead, perceived as akin to a female affinity with household items, fashion, and furniture, as in the case of Oppenheim's *Table with Bird's Legs* (1939), composed of a gilt wood tabletop imprinted with bronze bird legs, or her well-known *Bracelet with Fur* (1935).

Juxtaposing figural elements, material properties, and abstract or serialized formal vocabularies, Genzken's doll assemblages possess a kind of agency: subjects and objects blur boundaries between one another, as they are arranged in repetitive rows or made to seem somehow debilitated, inexplicably infirmed, or absurdly constrained; they may show signs of life but, almost as a rule, emit the restraining feeling of a predicament. They clearly have some "quality of life" issues. In this regard, the philosopher Eyal Chowers has helpfully surveyed some modern theories of entrapment associated with a deluded and deceived self, subjected to a "dehumanizing sameness that springs from the duplication of the social—the menace of homogenized existence in a world conceived of as self-made."[24] Entrapment writers tend to focus on institutional effects, in terms of how people are processed or "leveled" through increasingly automated cultures of calculative management— by formulating social policy, for instance, according to statistical bases for adjustments in workday hours, based on maximized output projections. Indeed one crucially immaterial context for Genzken's bluntly material and non-slick sculptural statement—displays that highlight (and denigrate) consumer objects, often playing down their novelty by absurdly and redundantly restating them in slightly different guises— is the intensification of prescriptive human behavior that has gone hand in hand with the evaporation of the tangible foundations for those prescriptions. Obedience to a transcendental entity or corporeal authority (e.g., a monarch) is displaced by obedience to commands whose origins are subjectless (i.e., bureaucratic and automated structures and systems). Within this technocratic and objectifying environment, the self may fail to determine the boundaries of its own authenticity, particularly when spoon-fed with seamlessly seductive imagery, presenting new consumer products as sources of fulfillment. This spoon-fed state goes hand in hand with self-denying behaviors: the remembered world

(*Merkwelt*) breaks up more quickly and the "mythic in it surfaces more quickly and crudely."[25]

I read Genzken's exhibition as a series of scenarios inhabited by an unseemly array of cobbled-together characters and props that stubbornly resist cohering into seamlessly packaged products. Fragmentary parts are forced into uneasy connections with abstract and material qualities, such as expanses of shiny foil, paint dribblings, briefcases, or packaging. There are many indications of neurotic and obsessive behaviors—often in tandem with some tragic signs of abuse—but it is indeed challenging to come to any confident conclusions about what stories are being told, and to what extent there is a centered, creative consciousness behind it all. And it is difficult to definitively say whether Genzken's repeated use of certain motifs, marks, and materials may serve as evidence of a consistent attempt at an aesthetic strategy, or the strategic outcome of a sincere (or soulful) artistic process. "OIL" in some sense critiques our increasing inability to engage in such a strategy. She addresses how we have become compromised by ideologies of technological progress and rampant consumerism—orchestrated by those who play games with our lives, and who put systems in play which result in the diminished capacity to empathize with each other (creatively or otherwise), so that we become like masked charlatans or mere monkeys hanging about. Or, despite the excitement of embracing electronic newness, we may be passively installed in a chair anchored to a wall, or suspended and floatingly weightlessly (or blindly, with the visor down) from a ceiling.

Genzken's work addresses a wide range of dehumanizing outcomes of living in an increasingly digitized and dematerialized world, including those associated with diminished creative and critical capacities associated with intimacy, with material production and people. In *The Soul at Work*, Franco Berardi offers an account of the recent mentalization of labor, and corresponding forms of alienation rooted in the subjugation of the self to work processes.[26] In particular, digital technologies have transformed the relation between conceiving and executing, and therefore the relation between the intellectual contents of labor and their manual execution. More and more, human workers enact simulations, which are later transferred to actual matter by computerized machines. The limits of "productive labor" become uncertain. For the cognitive worker every hour is not the same from the standpoint of produced value. And so labor loses a sense of material boundaries and "the productive activity only exerts its powers on what is left: symbolic abstractions, bytes and digits ..." Berardi defines an always-accelerating "mediasphere" as a de-eroticizing force that spreads competitive principles in every aspect of social life. Accordingly, he strives to come to terms with a new species of malaise associated with the "self becoming thing."[27] The human receiver is overtaxed by signifying impulses to the extent that he or she has a diminished ability to distinguish between metaphorical expression and literal communication. The infosphere causes social relations to shift from the analogical domain (of sizes, bodies, drives) to that of algorithms (relations, constants, simulations); digitization implies a shift at the essential level of manipulation, so that social products are no longer manipulated materially, but generated on a conceptual level. The pervasive spread of technologies of the invisible has caused a suppression of Protagoras's maxim, "man is the measure of all things." These days, generative algorithms count and determine the formation of social phenomena which no longer correspond closely to human measure, as the human eye can no longer perceive them. For Berardi, we are compelled to follow functional paths and submit to a chain of automatisms required by networked systems of operative exchanges, so that we literally become "terminals for the global mind."

Our souls are at the disposal of an immense immaterial factory, and our bodies lie flabbily at the borders of a playing field for Capital. Genzken's assemblage strategies may suggest such readings, but never in didactic or dogmatic ways. It is precisely because of such indirectness that I was able to have such a speculatively powerful encounter, experienced cumulatively in the Venice venue, allowing her arrangements to surprise me with the capacity to register as an urgent warning—about the consequences of unchecked greed, of exploiters playing games on a universal field.

Notes

1   Curated by Nicolaus Schafhausen, Genzken's exhibition was held at the Biennale di Venezia in 2007. My reading addresses a selective portion of the show.

2   Here I am thinking of the viscous black goo as a "character" that is granted generative (and malevolent) properties in the films *Prometheus* and in *The X Files*.

3   For discussion of some of these oil-related issues as they relate to narratives of progress and the notion of monumentality, see Andrew Apter, *The Pan-African Nation: Oil and the Spectacle of Culture in Nigeria* (Chicago: University of Chicago Press, 2005). See also Carl Boggs, ed., *Masters of War: Militarism and Blowback in the Era of American Empire* (New York: Routledge, 2003).

4   Merriam-Webster.com's primary definition of "self" is "*a*: the entire person of an individual, and *b*: the realization or embodiment of an abstraction."

5   The removal of swastikas and a Nazi eagle have been the only significant changes made to its imposing exterior since 1945.

6   In both title and form, Hans Haacke's work *Germania*, installed at the German Pavilion in 1993, contrasts well with Genzken's installation. Haacke broke up the marble floor, installed a photograph showing Hitler at the 1934

Biennale, hung a giant 1990 Deutschmark coin over the door, and repeated inside the pavilion the word "Germania"—the Italian term for Germany, but also Hitler's name for the Third Reich's redesigned capital city. Haacke's blatant and solemn focus on a single nation's crimes differs, I would argue, from Genzken's approach, which wavers between national and cultural contexts, and makes more room for ironic and satirical meaning.

7   For further discussion of Genzken's relationship to the pavilion, see Andrea Tarsia, "Oil," in Kasper König, Nina Gülicher, and Andrea Tarsia, eds., *Isa Genzken: Open Sesame!* (London: Koenig Books, 2009), 204–13. Tarsia offers one of only a few other detailed readings of Genzken's Venice show. In addition, see Lisa Lee, *Isa Genzken: Sculpture as World Receiver* (Chicago: University of Chicago Press, 2017), 5–8, 10–13, 102–05. Lee's book is the one of the most important and comprehensive studies of Genzken's work to date.

8   For comments on Genzken's Venice installation and its resistance to "all visual language that could be appropriated by national attributes of any kind," see Nicolaus Schafhausen's "Preface" to Schafhausen, ed., *Isa Genzken: Oil* (Cologne: DuMont Literatur und Kunst Verlag, 2007), 152.

9   See Didi-Huberman, *Confronting Images: Questioning the Ends of a Certain History of Art* (1990), trans. John Goodman (University Park, PA: Penn State University Press, 2005), 203.

10 Leo Steinberg once speculated, albeit momentarily, that Rauschenberg in this work may have been addressing the evolution of transportation technology (feet, tires, aviation), which Genzken also does, as we shall see.

11 See Leggio, "Robert Rauschenberg's *Bed* and the Symbolism of the Body," in John Elderfield, ed., *Essays on Assemblage: Studies in Modern Art 2* (New York: Museum of Modern Art, 1992), 79–117.

12 For Genzken, there also tends to be few one-off jokes, but rather multiple variations on a witty theme that depends on repetition, allowing for the extended play of irony. As with some of her peers, such as Rosemarie Trockel, there was a generational resistance to a "politics of realization," referencing politics without making commitments—avoiding direct action in favor of a more distanced, parodic skepticism associated with a "politics of potentiality." See the excellent discussion in Gregory H. Williams, *Permission to Laugh: Humor and Politics in Contemporary German Art* (Chicago: University of Chicago Press, 2012), 5, 14, 130–44. See also Linda Hutcheon, *A Theory of Parody: The Teachings of Twentieth-Century Art Forms* (Urbana and Chicago: University of Illinois Press, 1985), 52–53; and idem, *Irony's Edge: The Theory and Politics of Irony* (London and New York: Routledge, 1994), 25–27.

13 Mass media has replaced politicized existence as the new realm of democracy: increasingly, the media are in themselves seen as democratizers of culture, fully in the service of the illusion that the proliferation of commodities is tantamount to human liberation. Still the most perceptive and lucid discussion of these issues, from a Benjaminian perspective, is Susan Buck-Morss, *The Dialectics of Seeing: Walter Benjamin and the Arcades Project* (Cambridge, MA: MIT Press, 1989), 284, 359.

14 For good commentary on the dialectical relation of subject and object, and the role of projection and fantasy in the reception of Genzken's

recent work, see Juliane Rebentisch, "The Dialectic of Beauty: On the Work of Isa Genzken," in Nicolaus Schafhausen, ed., *Isa Genzken: Oil* (Cologne: DuMont Literatur und Kunst Verlag, 2007), 160–64. My speculative reading of "OIL" reflects Rebentisch's point that the "expressive" quality of Genzken's art requires the active accession of the viewer; it is only in the chains of association that grow out of specific works that it is "born into art" (162).

15 One final plinth supports an equally androgynous Oscar-style trophy—rendered in silver rather than gold—with the label "Isa Genzken, Best Director," a signatory gesture and perhaps an ironic reference to the Golden Lion awarded in Venice; like the skeletons, the trophy may be read as a tongue-in-cheek sign for a reckoning, a judgement by the powers that be, based on one's record, as an artist or a human being.

16 For discussion of the notion of travesty in Genzken's work, see Benjamin H. D. Buchloh, "All Things Being Equal: Isa Genzken," *Artforum* (November 2005): 222–25. Buchloh asserts that Genzken has confronted one of the prime calamities of sculpture these days: a terror that emerges from the universal equivalence and exchangeability of all objects and materials, and the "impossibility of imbuing any transgressive definition of sculpture with priorities or criteria of selection, of choice, let alone judgment (be it artisanal skills, choice of objects or materials, or the analytical intelligence to identify the specific structure of a contextualized readymade)" (224).

17 For comments on Genzken's relation to minimalism, see Alex Farquharson's survey account of the artist's career in Farquharson, ed., *Isa Genzken* (London: Phaidon, 2006).

18 See Graw's discussion of recent sculpture in Graw, Daniel Birnbaum, and Nikolaus Hirsch, eds., *Art and Subjecthood: The Return of the Human Figure in Semiocapitalism* (Berlin: Sternberg Press, 2011), 16–17. See also Horst Bredekamp, *Theorie des Bildakts* (Berlin: Suhrkamp Verlag, 2010), 47.

19 For treatment of the theme of violence in Genzken's doll assemblages, see for instance Barbara Engelbach, "Filming Children: Sculpture and Cinematic Space," in Kasper König, Nina Gülicher, and Andrea Tarsia, eds., *Isa Genzken: Open Sesame!* (London: Koenig Books, 2009), 186–91. See also Manisha Jothady, "Isa Genzken," *Art Papers* (January/February 2007): 87.

20 For perceptive and relevant comments on related works by Genzken, shown in a similarly sprawling installation at the Vienna Secession in 2006, see Lisa Lee, "Make Life Beautiful! The Diabolic in the Work of Isa Genzken (A Tour through Berlin, Paris, and New York)," *October* 122 (Fall 2007): 53–70. Particularly helpful are Lee's treatments of the lack of sculptural integrity and the notion of debilitation. For further discussion of the Vienna show, see Willem de Rooij, "Jump: Movement and Moving Image in Three Recent Installations by Isa Genzken," in Nicolaus Schafhausen, ed., *Isa Genzken: Oil*, 168–74.

21 These include Kurt Schwitters's *Der erste Tag Merz-Säule* (*First Day Merz Column*, 1923), an assemblage employing everyday imagery that was "playfully" topped by a baby's head resembling a child's doll, actually the plaster death mask of his infant son.

22 When the *Prussian Archangel* was exhibited in 1920 during the First International Dada Fair, the authorities charged the artists with defaming the German army.

23 For commentary, see Ingrid Pfeiffer, "Temporary Objects: Mannequins at the 1938 *Exposition international du surréalisme*," in Pfeiffer and Max Hollein, eds., *Surreal Objects: Three-Dimensional Works from Dali to Man Ray* (Frankfurt and Ostfildern: Schirn Kunsthalle Frankfurt and Hatje Cantz Verlag, 2011), 60–81.

24 Chowers, *The Modern Self in the Labyrinth: Politics and the Entrapment Imagination* (Cambridge, MA: Harvard University Press, 2004), 190.

25 In another gallery I observed three-legged objects resembling tables and stools—one mostly yellow, the other a mélange of hues—which have projections and other qualities which prevent use as seating. Straying from the utility of functional furniture, these sculptures emanate a sense of structural fragility and vulnerability, and they share space with a glassy construction made up of a pair of stacked, transparent cubes: each serves as plastic prison with a solitary wooden Russian doll inmate—combing hand-painted decoration with serial production—part of a set of nesting wooden figures of decreasing size, placed one inside the other. Here she is isolated from her kin, incarcerated; this architecture has a foil "latch," signifying that the door to the cube is ajar, and perhaps the occupants may be rescued. But the surface of this sculpture has indentations which create phantasmagorical interior effects, so that the female figurines seem ghost-like and immaterial. The rippled surface of these structures promotes transformations and projections that resonate with the notion of *mise en abyme* implicit in the Russian doll motif.

26 Berardi, *The Soul at Work: From Alienation to Autonomy*, trans. F. Cadel and G. Mecchia (Los Angeles: Semiotexte, 2009), 75, 135, 180–200. "Social labor time is like an ocean of value producing cells that can be grouped and recombined according to capital's needs" (191). Semiotic flows and circulation of goods overlap their codes, so that interpretation occurs according to endless spirals of associations and connections, and is less connected along sequential lines: what results is a greater sense of the irrelevant and the unintelligible. I am indebted to a compilation of essays, originally presented at a conference, devoted to debate and discussion about the potential relation of recent art to Berardi's notion of semiocapitalism: see Isabelle Graw, Daniel Birnbaum, and Nikolaus Hirsch, eds., *Art and Subjecthood: The Return of the Human Figure in Semiocapitalism* (Berlin: Sternberg Press, 2011).

27 Another feature of Berardi's "infosphere" is precariousness: digitized "info-labor" can be recombined in different locations, far from those actually producing it; for the cognitive worker, work tends to a fragmentary character, consisting of fractions of cellular time available for productive recombination at a later time and location, divorced from the worker's body. This system no longer recruits people in the traditional sense, but buys packets of de-personalized time, separated from their contingent bearers, who are regarded as interchangeable.

3 Geoffrey Farmer
"Me into Many"

Just outside the main galleries of the Musée d'art contemporain, Montréal, I am greeted by four sculptures placed precariously upon a dolly, presumably used by the museum's installation crews.[1] A most suitable entrée to a Geoffrey Farmer survey show, the dolly does double duty as pedestal and mobile stage—and it induces an ambivalence about whether those things on view are presented in their definitive, or even their intended, form. This platform serves as a provisional place for cobbled-together, humble assemblages that exemplify Farmer's penchant for portraying personages that are reductive and rudimentary to a provocative extent. A filled and tied plastic trash bag is placed next to a stack of wood hunks topped by a block with a pair of holes—an allusion to a head, with eyes rendered crudely with a drill, resulting in a subject and a self that are cracked and split, perhaps wooden as well. Sharing the stage is a cardboard box containing scraps of cut construction paper, maybe discarded while making the sort of frameable commodities on hand here. Perched on the opposite side is a faceless black-robed figure, with a wig of disheveled black hair. He/she holds a straw broom aloft, perhaps in preparation for flight, as a witch—or other shamanistic sort of being, present more in spirit than in body. Momentarily, the work comes across as a venue for the performance of unknown rituals, not tied to any institutional doctrine. As such, this stage may supply improvisational implements, articles to be adopted in order to invoke or to inhabit the souls of others. However, cutting into my scenario is a handwritten note, stuck to the gurney's steel railing: "Carl, just trying this out, take off if you need to use, G." At the outset, such abrupt juxtapositions—witch, note, bag, head, box—serve, along with Farmer's signatory sign ("G"), to signal a strategy seen throughout this exhibition: to signify incompleteness in a host of ways, and to offer indications of the artist's extended time spent on site, along with a resolute refusal to provide a display that seems seamlessly complete, or that can be summed up with ease as coherent curatorial product.

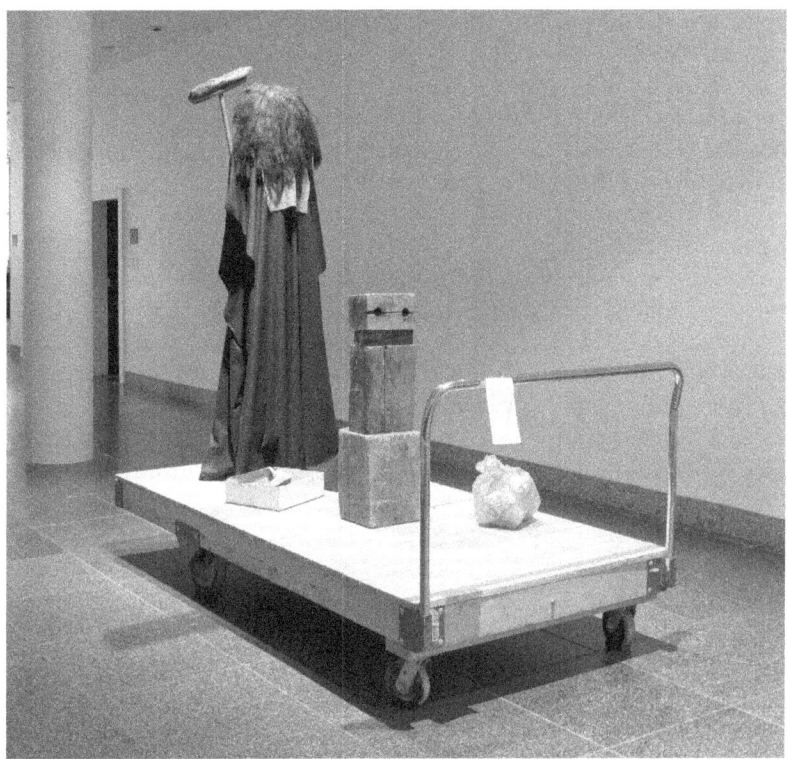

Figure 3.1 Geoffrey Farmer, *I am by nature one and also many, dividing the single me into many, and even opposing them as great and small, light and dark, and in ten thousand other ways*, 2001–2008

Wood, fabric, broom and wig, dimensions variable

Installation view, "Geoffrey Farmer," Musée d'art contemporain de Montréal, Montreal, QC, 2008

Photo: Guy L'Heureux. Courtesy of Catriona Jeffries, Vancouver

I soon learn from a wall label that the dolly assemblage is, in fact, part of a larger work—begun in 2001, and still unfinished—consisting of seven components dispersed throughout the exhibition. Its unwieldy title contains the phrase "dividing the single me into many," which I consider a nudging to seek out its other parts—fragments that collectively may add up to a self, an approximation of a person with qualities that may express how actual people designate and denigrate others.[2] As in a theatre of the absurd, Farmer composes characters and props that are inadequate as the cast and setting of a well-crafted and packaged (artistic) production.[3] Distinctly lacking in distinct characteristics, these compositions strive and struggle with predicaments that have no obvious origin or purpose, and which may be either permanent or provisional. Despite their dearth of specific qualities, they manage to provoke reactions of sympathy or empathy, partly because they have been placed and/or crafted with care by the artist, from modest materials, in remarkably spare ways. Farmer situates them, I would argue, in an allegorical manner, provoking speculation about how individuals become *reduced* to abstractions or objects—and conversely, how objects become personifications.

Near to the gurney is another portion of *I am by nature*: a mostly white assemblage resembling somebody reading the newspaper. Composed in an abruptly abbreviated manner, the body and head consist of a single Styrofoam block, with a degraded, weathered surface punctuated by dents, holes, and a few ruled lines. It is punctured by a pencil, sticking out where a mouth would be, a bit like a snowman's carrot. Again one hesitates to dwell, descriptively or aesthetically, on this figure's formal features: the foam has received marks that could be taken as signs of expressiveness, as slights, or as merely the result of damage during transport. But this subject has additional attributes: a masking tape roll is stuck to the top of its head, serving as a hat, another adornment that certainly qualifies as a product of the artist's hand, placed there like a dunce cap. But it is this subject's sense of predicament that comes across most strongly. The foam block rests on a mundane plastic chair that functions tentatively as pedestal and substitute for legs. A long florescent bulb is propped up against its immobilized body, referring to Dan Flavin's spare, monochrome sculptures of the early 1960s, which critiqued conventional and gestural signs of emotional expressiveness. Lastly, a crumpled two-page newspaper is taped to the armless body. Evoking an absurd sense of pathos, he or she appears to be perusing—or is forced to stare upon—a document that is blank, save for the header "Daily Times." There appears to be no news today, no stories populated by those with whom viewers may identify in comforting, anecdotal detail.

This paper-reading subject is treated in summarizing ways recalling the caricatured manner of some Dadaist imagery. George Grosz's watercolor drawing *Republikanische Automaten* (1920), for instance, depicts human figures that are similarly faceless, reductively rendered, and geometricized.[4] Grosz's hollow, gray-suited businessmen have their thoughts fed to them; their actions are prompted by mechanical gears, clearly conveying the utter emptiness of their gestures, like waving the German flag. Standing upon a peg leg, one man clutches the flag in a claw, while resting another handless arm on his hip. The number 12 appears on his face, suggesting he has been drawn from a herd of sheep, spewing patriotic cheers. Compared to Farmer's assemblages, Grosz's work was meant to satirize—in a relatively obvious way—those, including veterans, who blindly conformed to the centrist republic taking shape after the First World War.[5] Traditionally, satire is associated with an insistence on historical specificity—with words and images that are directed against specific individuals or social groups. Such satirical intent often is identified with the conveyance of chastisement or ridicule.[6] While Farmer's Daily-Times character does seem caricatured—and potentially disabled or incapacitated—it is far from certain whether this portrayal of a person is meant as a mean-spirited mocking of anyone in particular. Indeed, Farmer's personages are peculiar: they possess qualities and attributes, but cannot be pinned down. Often, they signify a provisional *process* of performing or composing a character—out of cast-off materials that are simply at hand or seemingly inadequate for satisfying storytelling.[7]

Relevant in this regard is a Dada context of assemblage that incorporates fragmented representations of dolls, tailor's heads, and dummies—in the service of portraying modern subjects that have been compromised or hollowed out by ideologies of mechanization and commodification. Sophie Taeuber's series of painted wooden *Dada Heads* (from the late 1910s and early 1920s), for example, parody the historic traits of portrait busts. Her works were turned on a lathe, and made up of geometric fragments such as ovoids, trapezoids, cones, and cylinders. As Hal Foster has discussed, they were made during a time when the relation between people and objects was becoming less clear. As with Taeuber, Farmer's figures signify a sense of diminishing agency and constrained identity but may be further identified, despite their industrial qualities (the product of a mechanical lathe or made up of packing material), with private situations of playing and making. Farmer's figures, however, still retain a relationship to the history of envisioning marionettes, dummies, and dolls as iconic characters associated with godly grace and uncanny power—rather than solely with the negativity of a Dada predicament resulting from mechanistic oppression. Farmer's sculptural characters should not be solely read as reflective of alienation in its most dire forms, a thematic thread that ends, in a sense, with Beckett's *Endgame* (1957), which features vegetative characters awaiting death.

Nearby, visitors are invited to enact a non-skilled performance with *Ghost Face* (2008). Here the artist employs a hollowed-out column: a person may enter inside, step onto a box and peer out through two holes, as though the column momentarily serves as a mask, observing others wandering about the exhibit, likely unaware of the surveillance. Farmer's forms of staging may bring about a critical awareness of conventional museum-going experiences, in which visitors co-inhabit a space, eyeing one another, with varying degrees of empathy. Or as the title implies, visitors might prefer to read the performer as installed within the column as a spirit, either one who haunts the public or is possessed momentarily by the museum's resident poltergeist. Or they might playfully occupy the role of an institutional authority, surveying formerly fellow visitors to develop a better educational or marketing strategy. This range of identities complicates any specific satirical aspects that may motivate Farmer's remarkably simple (but far from simplistic) architectural intervention—as a mocking of the museum. The ritual of donning masks is a tried and true tool of the sneaky satirist. We are conditioned to suspect the motives of the disguised character, poised to perform insults with anonymous abandon—with the deliberate dash and excess of a parodist, or with the intention of wreaking havoc and taunting the system. But in Farmer's hands the parodist dances between the poles of performer and watcher, possessor and possessed, those playing ironic tricks and those doing magic.[8] There is the potential to playfully *inhabit* the role of a masquerader, or to solemnly become *inhabited* by something else.

Worth recalling in this regard is Belgian author Maurice Maeterlinck's visionary, Symbolist mode of theatre, which depended on absurdity in ways that are resonant for Farmer's practice. For *The Blue Bird* (1908), actors imagined themselves as a loaf of bread or a tree, reflecting a notion of striving to sense things as they are—or how they might seem— to the eye of innocence, a viewing with simple immediacy. Indeed actors in *The Blue Bird* were trained to imagine themselves into nonhuman modes of being, studying the individuality of an animal or trying to feel themselves limited to one essential attribute: the sweetness of sugar, the flow of water. The comical incidents associated with these gestures were not meant to be merely cynical or satirical jokes.

I turn away from *Ghost Face*, moving into a darkened space that further reflects Farmer's contentment with character content that is unresolved and fluid. The video installation *The Fountain People* (2008) features footage of a fountain found at the base of an escalator, likely in an upscale shopping center.[9] Waiting in vain for the narrative to flow further—feasibly featuring the people mentioned in the title—viewers must make do with the banal sight of gushing water spouts, the dull glow of underwater lights, and the sedating stream of mall music. This is a scene of utterly banal homogeneity, portraying a place designed deliberately to encourage the uncritical consumption of standardized products. And it is an ideal setting for challenging preconceptions about what constitutes an artistically expressive event. And yet the video's benign imagery becomes a backdrop for a theatrical scenario—of being watched and manipulated by unknown forces—supplied by a few typewritten pages pinned to the wall, providing vague references to aquatic forces that are covertly monitoring, surrounding, and morphing. According to

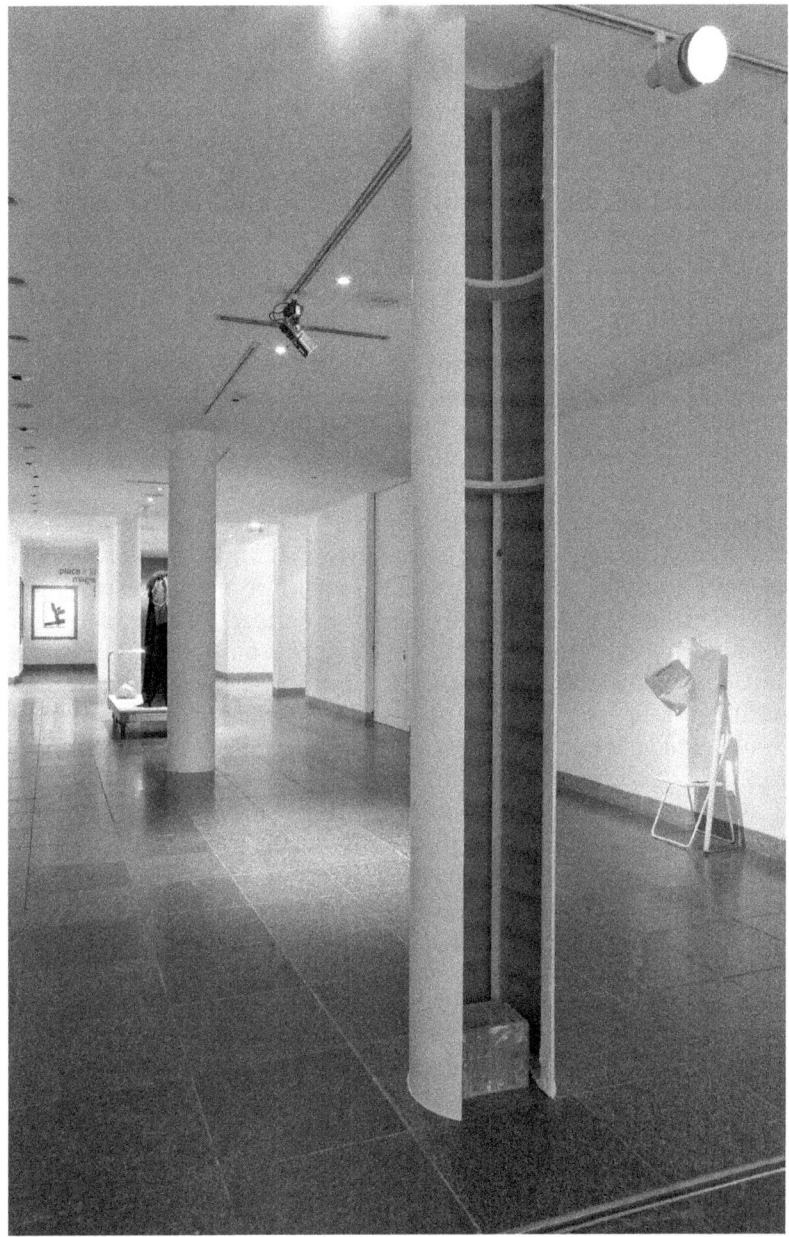

Figure 3.2 Geoffrey Farmer, *Ghost Face*, 2008

Cardboard form, wood, cotton, glue, eyes cut out of post and a standing shelf, 157 × 20 in. (398 × 50 cm)

Installation view, "Geoffrey Farmer," Musée d'art contemporain de Montréal, Montreal, QC, 2008.

Photo: Guy L'Heureux. Courtesy of Catriona Jeffries, Vancouver

this posting, the more people ingest and bathe using this ubiquitous resource, the more powerful "they" become. With these words, I arrive at some surprising associations, including scenes in Stanley Kubrick's *Dr. Strangelove* about a communist conspiracy accomplished through the fluoridation of bodily fluids, and the Pretenders song verse "And muzak filled the air from Seneca to Cuyahoga Falls." But then suddenly, while anticipating narrative incidents on screen, a slight (non) event does, in fact, occur: the muzak momentarily ceases, and suddenly a bit of smoky exhaust escapes from a vent. This may be evidence of the otherworldly "they" and their ability to transform. The onscreen spouts of water do take on the appearance of a group of humanoid beings, gathering and gushing, watching and emanating, in ways that are not fully fathomable. Offering up these lowly bits of paper and footage, Farmer manages to play effectively with the conditioning of visitors, with their hunger for the packaged products and plots populating the polished floors of venues, from malls to museums.

Entering the main gallery, many visitors would be conditioned to crave a display subscribing to the established norms of staging a mid-career survey, starring a "Geoffrey Farmer" convincingly and coherently portrayed—using the tried and true methods of the linear, developmental narrative. This would begin, so the formula goes, with a section revealing the protagonist's background and early influences, and would gradually lead up to mature, resolved, original works that *have* true importance and import.

A titanic *Trailer* (2002) appears as a thirty-foot-long film industry production vehicle, used commonly for hauling equipment such as props and costumes. But upon closer examination, it is revealed to be a fabricated shell, made mostly of fiberboard and steel. A portrait of a machine meant to move at substantial speed, this trailer approximation registers as passive and fragile. It has been denied resilience and locomotion. Crafted non-industrially, the work comes across as a haunted, enormously blank abstraction, an empty vessel with an undefined subjectivity that asks to be articulated according to its surroundings—as a prop.

This inert and hollow thing thus is good company, or perhaps home, for the pair of spectral personages—other members of the *I am by nature* cast of characters—standing close by. Containing a plywood coat-rack-like structure as a seemingly short-term skeleton, one wears a hooded jacket that cannot serve as a supplier of warmth, as it has been shredded into slender strips resembling a tribal headdress. Protruding from the tattered garment is a broom, held aloft in a manner akin to a flag, banner, or some other ceremonial instrument. However, a length of black masking tape extends from the broom's top to a tape roll on the floor—a feature that serves to discourage mobility, as in the case of the engine-less, torpid trailer. I read Farmer's figure as a *basic being* that is being subjected to a ritualized process of character construction, a performative act with some procedural requirements: the implements and attributes must be lacking in preciousness and simple in nature. Currently, he or she cannot (yet) register as a complete, coherent, or centered self, but can come across as *someone and/or something on display, as an exhibit or embodiment of difference*—to the institution, to the gods, to the spirit world, or to the gaze of others.

Farmer's project is reminiscent of Hannah Höch's series of collages *From an Ethnographic Museum* (1925–30), which employs a strategy of juxtaposing fragmentary components—drawn from divergent sources—signaling, with remarkably humble means, a range of genders, ethnicities, and other traits within a single cobbled-together personage. In *Monument II: Vanity* (1926), for instance, Höch's androgynous figure is composed of multiple magazine snippets. Standing in *contrapposto* against a background of pink and blue colored papers, his/her head wears an African mask featuring a fanned headdress.[10] Farmer's figures also provoke a sense of disorientation or discomfort that comes from not being able to efficiently categorize singular identities. One may unexpectedly feel a sense of sympathy, or at least empathy, for his hybridized (anti)characters, pinned down to the floor, forced to play the immobile role of statues.

Close-by stands an armless figure—resembling a tailor's dummy—wearing an old-fashioned and modest blouse and skirt. Placed on her head is a torn and crumpled box, its cardboard surfaces serving as a degrading display site for some abstract drawings, affixed with scotch tape. She recalls Dada performances at the Cabaret Voltaire, in which artists would costume themselves with geometric pieces of cardboard, often inhibiting movement, while interacting with tailor's dummies.[11] The box may be read as part of a process of subjection, a humbling and perhaps humiliating erasure of individuality. Her person has literally become the backdrop for a mini show. And it has been done in a fashion suggesting the broader process of losing ego and self-worth to the degree that one may become inhabitable, worn, or possessed by others—mentally, spiritually, or literally—as a performative prop.[12] The figure also wears a crystal pendant, which may aid in such acts of possession. But along with this more metaphysical context, I would argue that the work may be read in terms of earthly social rituals surrounding shame. As Agnes Heller has discussed, shame may occur among the domesticated and socialized, as it is a social affect that is triggered by an authority, either absent or immediately present.[13] An ashamed subject may, for instance, imagine a future judgment of "abnormality" or recall a past memory of being labeled "impure." The bearer of the social triggers of shame is most often the eye of the community,

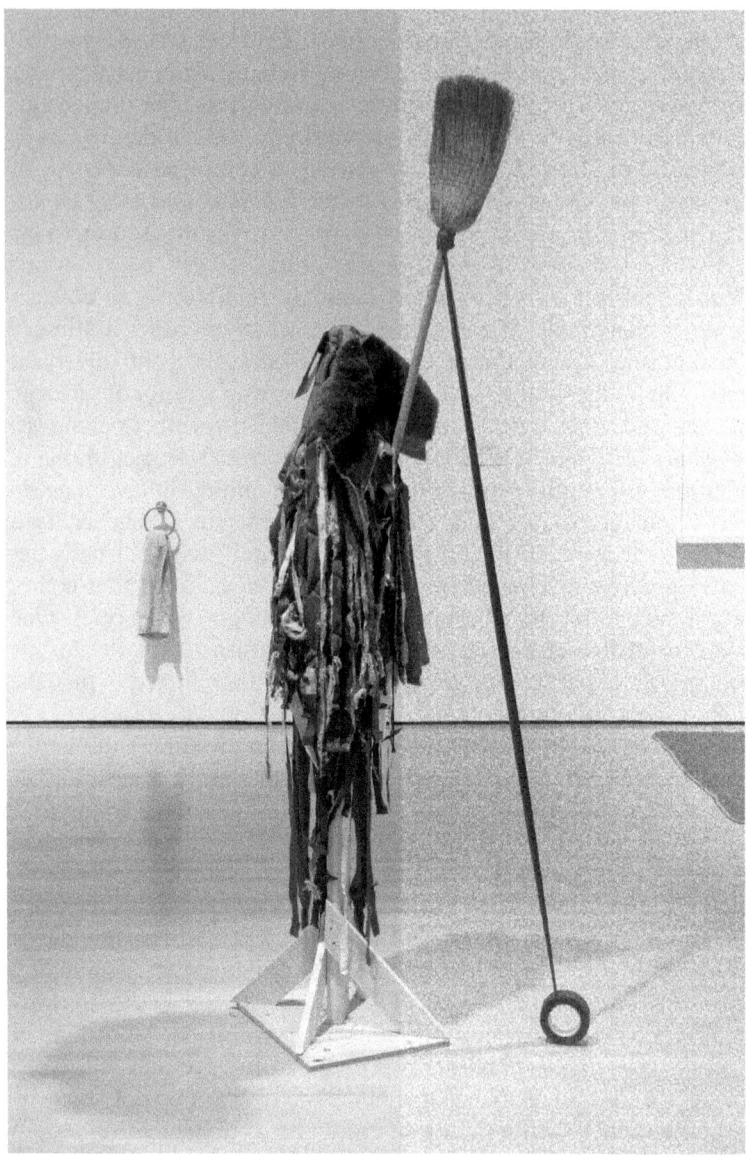

Figure 3.3 Geoffrey Farmer, *I am by nature one and also many, dividing the single me into many, and even opposing them as great and small, light and dark, and in ten thousand other ways*, 2001–2008

Wooden post, black tape, broom, shredded jacket from *Rambo* movie, 45 rpm record sleeve, 93 × 32 × 32 in. (236 × 81 × 81 cm)

Installation view, "Geoffrey Farmer," Musée d'art contemporain de Montréal, Montreal, QC, 2008

Photo: Guy L'Heureux. Courtesy of Catriona Jeffries, Vancouver

but the shamed self feels that she is constantly on display no matter what she is doing. People exposed to shame because of their ostensible differences may also be exposed to laughter and mocking. If she visibly carries out activities according to the norms of a community, one avoids shame, and the Eye approves. But there is also shame that derives from an inner conscience, as a personal voice that may only seem a vague intuition, from a source which cannot be pinpointed in time or place. In the latter case, if she imagines infringing on rules—or constructs herself as different—she may then become "possessed" by shame, blushing or adopting disguises in order to avoid being seen. The prevailing feeling may be one of vulnerability.

Farmer's (non)protagonists perform semantic slides back and forth between the conditions of thing and personage, object and subject. As such they are abstractions, presiding and witnessing like (anti)monuments that do not project pride or glory. Cut off at the knees or shoulders, they may serve as tragic or pathetic signs for an absence of ego or integrity—of either the physical or moral variety—yet manage to retain a lively innocence, while denying the grandeur associated with traditions of representing people with importance, such as heroic portraiture and statuary, and their attendant iconographies of the ego. Indeed Farmer's figures sport few features that may serve to signify social status and learnedness. As such they could also come across negatively—as reminders, or mementos, of what people may become: faceless automatons.

Mostly made up of myriad packing, kitchen, and office materials, Farmer's *Entrepreneur Alone Returning Back to Sculptural Form* (2002) is an expansive conglomeration of disposable stuff, manipulated and distributed with a great deal of delicate care, reflecting an extended period of on-site enterprise, as the title suggests.[14] An enormous disc consisting of regular rows of yellow Post-It notes has been patiently applied to the wall, one note at a time. This sun may be a provisional part of an inexpensive stage set—and a celestial cue to consider the idea that the sheer laborious accumulation of identical motifs, simply arranged as a circle, is an artistic statement in itself. Post-Its are a means to jot down tasks or thoughts, serving as reminders of things to be acted upon later, or eventually forgotten. Normally considered supplemental in importance at best, they are often imminently expendable, stuck to larger things such as screens, desks, refrigerators. Farmer's notes are all blatantly blank, however, and hence have yet to be occupied by ideas. They may represent a lack of inspiration, or absence of any need to recollect. However, the Post-It sun shines on much other material made after the Entrepreneur's return: a collection of crumpled-up pieces of paper is placed atop and around a trash can, perhaps further signifying the repeated failure, or flirtation, with finding inspiration—for a marketable idea or "branding" experience suitable for the entrepreneur to stage. Indeed, placed in the same gallery corner—as if in temporary storage in a studio—are office supplies and a bunch of in-progress artworks propped up against walls, along with a lit desk lamp, casting a glow over a mundane office chair, and a cardboard box containing plant-like forms made of foil. The box is set atop two floor-based monitors that face each other. Both screens play a video of someone producing these aluminum flora with feet—a display of agility to be sure, but also conceivably meant to suggest how art functions as fetish.

Another part of *Entrepreneur* features a pair of boots, perhaps prepared for the hardworking feet seen in the video, composed of socks and packing tape. This footwear would potentially serve as protective covering for someone destitute—a humiliating thing for a person to wear that might lower him or her to the condition of an anonymous abstraction. One boot stands on a plastic pail, a humble plinth suggesting the tentative notion, rather than reality, of memorializing or paying heed to this comic-tragic character as a statue, stationed with a single leg raised, for posterity. But of course, I could adopt this footwear as a prop—maybe as a means to momentarily inhabit this identity, or somehow make it my own. When slipping on the boots, a visitor might grab a shovel situated nearby, and do a bit of digging upon inspecting an opening in the wooden floor, a hole that reveals wiring. Textile strips hang down from another square-shaped opening in the ceiling, further revealing the institution's internal physiology, aspects not normally visible within the staged museum experience. Or someone might pick up a long sinuous strip of cloth, loosely gathered on the ground, perhaps a homemade measuring tape needed to confirm distance excavated. A thoroughly weathered piece of brown paper hangs on the wall, adorned only with two oval holes for the eyes; this could be worn as well, as an immature means of masquerade.

In the realm of theatre, spectators confronting a performance from a safe distance may be ignorant about the processes and realities behind onstage appearances.[15] To spectate in this traditional sense is to be separated from the capacity to know and the ability to act.[16] For Bertolt Brecht and other avant-gardists, theatre was reconceived as an outlet for the aesthetic constitution of a community, a sensible constitution of bodies in action, a set of perceptions, gestures, and attitudes that make up experience and that precede political institutions. Farmer's display serves as a setting that posits a potential for progressive, performative participation, employing commonplace props and activities. Such performances may offer an outlet to consider the capacity of ordinary, anonymous people, a capacity that makes everyone equal, a capacity exercised by an unpredictable interplay of associations and dissociations within the here and now of the gallery space. One of Brecht's earliest

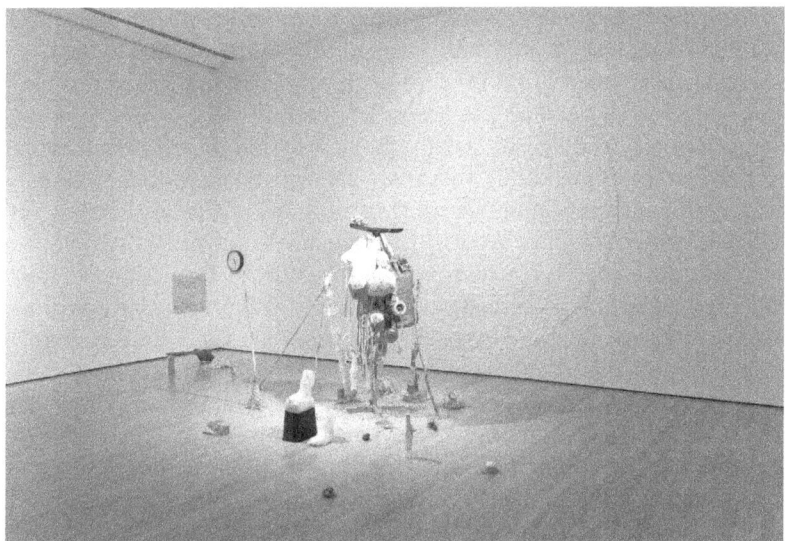

Figure 3.4 Geoffrey Farmer, *Entrepreneur Alone Returning Back to Sculptural Form*, 2002
Mixed media, dimensions variable
Installation view, "Geoffrey Farmer," Musée d'art contemporain de Montréal, Montreal, QC, 2008. Photo: Guy L'Heureux. Courtesy of Catriona Jeffries, Vancouver

plays, *In the Jungle of the Cities* (1924), required that the director and crew remove barriers that would normally hide backstage areas. Instead of conventional footwear, black boots were painted on the actors' feet. During the performance, stagehands and actors could be seen milling around in the background, and for extra effect, a door to the theatre was opened before the play and during intermission, allowing the audience to view street traffic. Such incidental details, composed with seeming spontaneity on a shoestring budget, as it were, proliferated in Brecht's productions, as one means to stray from conventions of the well-made play. And his non-actors performed "purposeless" and repetitive on-stage activities, gestures akin to making dozens of aluminum flora, or placing a profusion of blank Post-Its on a wall.

At the heart of *Entrepreneur* are masking tape rolls, tattered strips of cloth, plastic shopping bags, paper cups, and much else—all subjected to processes of filling up, taping, piling, stretching, or gluing. But in one spot they have congregated to make up a massive figure with centralized innards, yet somewhat dispersed by multiple layers of bolstering devices, tripods, and columnar forms. This figure may be read as the Entrepreneur, caught up in a predicament: this being has been battered, beleaguered, and weighed down, literally and metaphorically. The burdened subject's array of appendages and long limbs may seem structurally necessary to keep him or her upright—or may signify the process of reaching or striving in vain for mobility or social contact. Worth recalling in this regard are some of Samuel Beckett's theatrical personages, reflecting his effort to rid plots of linear causality, yet without obliterating characters.[17] Like Farmer's infirmed Entrepreneur, Beckett's protagonists often appear on the verge of extinction, severely inhibited, sometimes confined to wheelchairs. And yet they have a recognizable integrity: they strive to maintain themselves over time, to simply carry on, and this is enhanced by the reductive immediacy and stark materiality of their performances. Despite the composition's dispersed appearance, Farmer's centralized character does signify the status of a personage, while semantically sliding from subject to object, while also suggesting the practical process of demonstrating the tensile and supportive strengths of commonplace materials, like plastic bags. This disorienting display exhibits a diversity of texture and form, enriched by scattered bits of pink tissue paper, socks, fake pearls, and even a hummingbird, hiding amongst the profusion of non-preciousness. And yet, details are denied the chance to become a focused, plot-oriented preoccupation. Clumps of tape are liberally spread throughout, sometimes as a means of securing stuff, like a bottle, to the floor. And the tape serves as sticky signs of the residue of preparing and transporting the sort of precious products that are seldom seen in Farmer's work: commodities with value in the conventional sense. It is difficult to imagine a more mundane substance than beige packing tape. A single clump has been applied to a peripheral section of the floor. It stands alone, more isolated than any other element.[18] It propositions visitors, slyly saying: "I dare you to find value in me, or in the way I relate to my surroundings. Just try to find worth here."[19]

In describing or designating such peripheral properties, I recall Roland Barthes's famous treatment of Gustave Flaubert, particularly how he discussed the room occupied by the character of Madame Aubain, Félicité's mistress.[20] Flaubert mentions items placed on an old piano, including a barometer standing atop boxes and cartons. Flaubert's notations are focused on descriptive details that would normally be considered superfluous to the main articulations of narrative structure: they are fillers, padding, provided only to cumulatively add flavor to the sense of atmosphere. These notations were in a sense scandalous because they are "useless": they increase the "cost" of narrative information. The boxes may signify disarray but the barometer seems not to belong to the domain of the notable. Some details do not come across as being predictive, but rather as analogical or purely additive. Higher languages have a component that is not justified by any purpose of action, or communication. In discussing Flaubert, Barthes posits the idea of an additive description with no limits—to the extent that for the reader it reaches the realm of absurdity—when it is no longer guided and limited by the imperatives of the story. There is no indication why the chain of descriptive detail should stop at a particular point according to an aesthetic or rhetorical imperative: "… there would always be some corner, some detail, some nuance of location or colour to add."[21] Indeed, Barthes speaks of a measured amount of redundant words, insignificant objects, and transitory attitudes as a means to remain true to authentic experience.

Farmer's *Actor / Dancer / Carver* (2003) is a video installation depicting footage taken while wearing a basket on the head, wooden and padlocked boxes on the hands, and a rope fastened around the legs while wandering through a playground and a park.[22] The basket/mask covers human eyes, but contains a hole through which the camera stares. The work evokes a comical premise, associated with slapstick stunts, as this character confronts a wire mesh fence, playground paraphernalia, and a cedar bush. The pace is much slower and plodding compared to Vaudeville gags or the masochistic antics of the television show *Jackass*.[23] Farmer's brand of humor is absurd, self-deprecating, and inflected again by acts of ego erasure, either self-imposed or enforced by some other person or institution. The performer's identity is not known. The basket, with handles heavily covered in bright yellow tape, inhibits perception—as was the case with the cardboard box on the head of the female figure—to the extent that the unknown bearer of these props may be imperiled. This hazard is suggested when he/she bumps into a bush. The video, the basket, and a sketch for the work are displayed in the gallery on a mover's blanket, along with a length of rope of the sort that might be employed suicidally—thus adding a touch of morbidity and pathos, provoking my speculation that this recorded performance is the evocation of a life that is aimless, ashamed, purposeless, and perhaps controlled (or menaced) by an invisible force. This force may be societal, internal, metaphysical, or magical in nature.[24]

However, these humble objects lying in the gallery are an invitation to anyone—to put them on, to adapt them their own purposes and desires, perhaps in response to Farmer's video. For instance, these props might assist me with signifying a spirited condition of disability, rather than doomed aimlessness or foolish self-endangerment. Rather than being subjected to a tragic condition of being compelled to perform hopeless gestures, I may *choose* to stumble along while so inhibited, striving to chart a path, wavering between faith in my course and doubt about whether there is value to be had in this strange ritual. I may try

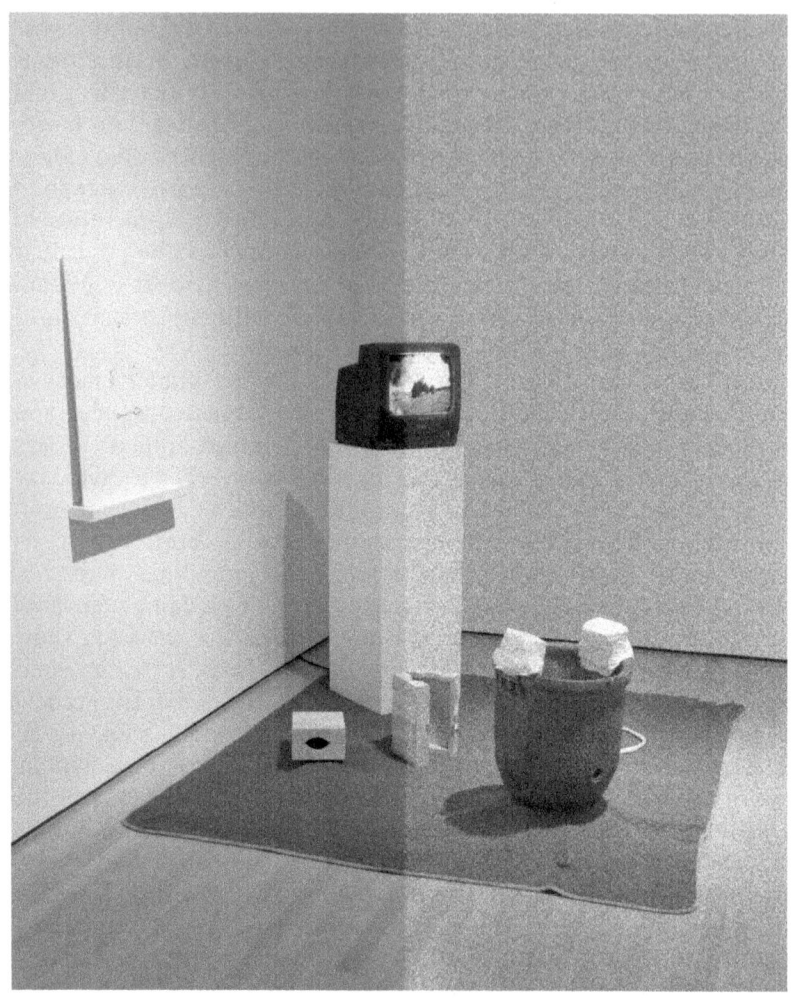

Figure 3.5 Geoffrey Farmer, *Actor / Dancer / Carver*, 2003

Lightjet print, basket, wood, rope, VHS video loop, video camera, monitor, various materials, dimensions variable

Installation view, "Geoffrey Farmer," Musée d'art contemporain de Montréal, Montreal, QC, 2008

Photo: Guy L'Heureux. Courtesy of Catriona Jeffries, Vancouver

to perform within or out of (or perhaps profit from) my predicament—which I could have freely adopted or had imposed upon me—with all of its physical inhibitions, constraints, and potential dangers. Ultimately, I might take pride in the idea that my gestures may lead some spectators—within a park or maybe a museum—to label me as unbalanced, unfocused, or not getting with the program.

Germano Celant coined the term *Arte Povera* in 1967, inspired by the "poor theatre" conceived by Jerzy Grotowski, which sought to return theatrical performance to origins associated with cathartic ritual and collective representation.[25] Theatre, it was thought, should not try to compete with the richness of film or television, or with the technical and artificial splendors of other media. Accordingly, it was necessary to pare down all forms of theatrical mediation, focusing on the "actor" as the primary element, or Actor/Dancer/Carver in Farmer's case. This required a paring down of the art object to an elementary set of "poor" propositions and gestures (stumbling along, reading a blank newspaper, holding a broom aloft). Mostly based in Turin and Rome, some Arte Povera artists did envision the gallery as a stage-like space, where fact and fiction are joined in a "theatrical" suspension of judgment. The goal of conveying an "impoverished" vision was achievable by gradually freeing the artistic setting from layers of ideological preconceptions, from the norms and rules of language and narrative—and an overall decrease of intellectual control over experience (*deculturare*). These artists tended to compose on a human scale, juxtaposing mundane manufactured materials (tape, monitor) with organic natural elements (basket, rope). The avant-garde principles of innovation, originality, and advancement were considered little more than mimicry of capitalist strategies and cultures of novelty. Rather, poetic statements were sought, with simple and reductive means in contrast with artistic tendencies overly concerned with end results: autonomous goods divorced from the processes that led to them. And there of course was a mystical side to the Arte Povera project as well, identified with conveying "primary energies," corresponding with physical forces (gravity or friction) and with fundamental aspects of human nature (vitality, memory, emotion).

Reflecting further on Farmer's range of rudimentary masks, torsos, and heads—made of mere crumpled paper bags, a split wooden block, low-grade footage of a mall fountain, or the like—it is important to reflect on the notion of magical discourse, tied to hidden knowledge of how everyday things can be made to speak, or brought to life, taking on talismanic roles which have more to do with their ritualistic placement, treatment, and potential activation by a group of participants. As Jan Verwoert has discussed, magical phenomena may allow for an understanding, rather than an explanation, of the material dimension of how social relations are forged, because they go beyond empirical representation, reaching into the realm of performance. Magical or mystical rites are not conventionally categorized as productive forms of labor, but they do determine "workable ways of relating to the living environment (as a metaphysical whole) in everyday practice, in a manner that allows for mundane acts to mediate spiritual concerns, and vice versa."[26] While institutions cannot be allowed to validate or regulate this activity, people must be able to maintain the ability to play (or imagine playing) such roles in an open-ended manner— a method that runs the risk of meeting with the social designation of otherness associated with the ridiculous, the embarrassing, or even the shameful. Such speculations and antics resist the marketing-oriented transformation of the spaces of sculptural experience—by employing descriptive language derived from sociology or interior design contexts, prioritizing the power of spatial ambience over the magic of the thing—via social networks that follow a

> technocratic logic, because the devices and scripts employed for electronic communication literally make *activating* and *administrating* relationships the same operation (as contacts, messages, and mails instantly become data organized in the digital archives of smart phones and personal computers).[27]

And yet, thinking again of the Entrepreneur forming foil plants, the Daily-Times figure, and other Farmer onstage personalities encountered earlier, I am compelled to come back to Beckett. As Anna McMullan has discussed, Beckett's later plays absurdly critique—and sometimes parody or mock—conventional attempts to frame human existence as something representable. His staged personas are mainly immobile, and yet they register past activities, as bodies showing signs of wear, of legacies of cultural inscription, and of dehumanizing abuses or neglect. Accordingly, there is a lack (but never an absence) of presence "that is both the predicament of these particular creatures, and the exposure of a coercive grammar of identity and authority that judges and condemns all who are wanting."[28] Beckett's *Play* (1962) reflects a greater denaturalization of the actor's body and a formal patterning of all elements of the *mise-en-scène* that undermine perceptual stability: delivery of the voice, movement, gesture, spoken text, space, light, and sound. Both male and female characters are defined by their corporeal needs, desires, or compulsions to accumulate or hoard or consume, rather than performing a fulfilling lifestyle for others: Pozzo requires chicken, while Hamm requires painkillers. They may also be defined by their dysfunctions or disabilities, such as blindness or lack of mobility. As with Farmer's, Beckett's figures are frequently placed in positions of vulnerability, states of deterioration, and dependence, emphasizing a difference in identity from traditional performances of "heroic" masculinity which exclude or repress those experiences. Props tend to serve such purposes in all of Beckett's theatre: the tree, stone, and mound in *Waiting for Godot*, for instance. Sometimes these things are used as prosthetic devices, but they frequently serve to emphasize decreased agency or limit perception in some way.[29]

As with Beckett's, Farmer's tainted characters persist and persevere, despite the restrictions and embarrassments. As anonymous actors, they enact their activities of "difference" within a public sphere, conceived as a theatre of identity and character formation. These enactments have an absurd flavor, given what they rub up against: forms of determinism that rule societies so enthralled with fulfilling consumerist needs. Some see no hope of become freed from the dehumanizing effects of institutions, and so the best they can do is cope, devising ways of surviving by recovering and asserting their singular selves, yet always in a partial and fragmentary sense. This is a continual struggle because they live in a world in which the intensification of prescriptive human behavior goes hand in hand with the evaporation of the tangible foundations of those prescriptions. Obedience to a transcendental entity or corporeal authority is displaced by obedience to commands whose origins are subjectless.[30]

Employing a host of techniques, including absurdist humor, provocatively humble materials, caricature, and abbreviation, I see Farmer engaging in a dialogue with display strategies employed in theatre museum, and retail culture, forging characters and productions which express a sense of wonder, of comic incomprehension, and of tragic misalignment with the world. With its relentless promotion of novel, new commodities, the capitalist machine disguises this lack, portraying products, including blockbuster exhibitions, as distractions providing temporary and illusory feelings of fulfillment. I would claim that if Farmer could believe in clearly defined motivations, acceptable solutions, settlements of conflict, and tidily tied-up endings, he would certainly not eschew them. But there are no clear-cut beliefs, no stable scale of values, and no ethical system in full working order. In the wake of wars and other atrocities, the absurdist sees the world as having ceased to make sense. Explanations of meaning have been unmasked as nonsensical illusions, empty chatter. Farmer envisions a dramaturgy populated by things in uncannily strange—and at times anthropomorphic—configurations, creating situations in which what makes sense at one moment has, at the next, become an obscure babble of foreign voices. This sense of isolation and difference must inevitably lead to a questioning of the recognized instrument for the communication of meaning: language.

Notes

1 Curated by Pierre Landry, Farmer's exhibition was held at the Musée d'art contemporain de Montréal (2008). My reading addresses a selective portion of the show.

2 The full title is *I am by nature one and also many, dividing the single me into many, and even opposing them as great and small, light and dark, and in ten thousand other ways.*

3 For an imaginative treatment of encounters with sculptural personages in Farmer's work, see Jan Verwoert, "A Mask, a Mouth and the Light (As It Fades)," in Heike Munder, et al., eds., *Geoffrey Farmer: Let's Make the Water Turn Black* (Zurich: Migros Museum für Gegenwartskunst and JRP Ringier, 2013), 67–70. For crucial comments on Farmer's approach to staging and props, see Diedrich Diederichsen, "Time (Lost in Flight) Regained," in Zoë Gray, Nicolaus Schafhausen, and Monika Szewczyk, eds. *Geoffrey Farmer: Forgetting Air* (Rotterdam: Witte de With, 2008), 7–15: "Farmer has no interest in the classical tactics used to terrify children by means of making inanimate things come to life, or subjectivizing objects (which in any event is now the daily fare of advertising). Instead he is interested in seeing the background become the central event *as background*, without being stripped of its defining characteristics: a tendency to remain behind, to enable, and to make itself available as a metonymic extension" (11). For further discussion of this enabling aspect, see below.

4 For interesting comments on Grosz's relationship to avant-garde German theatrical culture, including Brecht, see Herbert Knust, "George Grosz: Literature and Caricature," *Comparative Literature Studies* 12, no. 3 (1975): 218–47. For some relevant discussion of caricature within the Berlin Dada context, see Brigid Doherty, "Figures of the Pseudorevolution," *October* 84 (Spring 1998): 64–89.

5 For the leftist Grosz, the Weimar Republic had betrayed the workers and radicals responsible for overthrowing the empire.

6 For relevant treatment of these issues, see for instance John R. Clark, "Vapid Voices and Sleazy Styles," in Brian A. Connery and Kirk Combe, eds., *Theorizing Satire: Essays in Literary Criticism* (New York: St. Martin's Press, 1995), 19–42.

7 See Foster, "Philosophical Toys and Psychoanalytic Travesties: Anthropomorphic Avatars in Dada and the Bauhaus," in Isabelle Graw, Daniel Birnbaum, and Nikolaus Hirsch, eds., *Art and Subjecthood: The Return of the Human Figure in Semiocapitalism* (Berlin: Sternberg Press, 2011), 20–33.

8 For helpful discussion, see Robert Elliott, *The Power of Satire: Magic, Ritual, Art* (Princeton: Princeton University Press, 1960).

9 For further comments on this work, see my review in *Artforum* (September 2008).

10 For further discussion of this series, see Maud Lavin, "The Mess of History or the Unclean Hannah Höch," in Catherine de Zegher, ed., *Inside the Visible: An Elliptical Traverse of 20th Century Art* (Cambridge, MA: MIT Press, 1996), 117–24.

11 Also pertinent is the performance piece "Greatest-Ever-DADA-Show," held at the Saal zur Kaufleuten, Zurich, on April 9, 1919. With sets designed by Hans Arp and Hans Richter, the "cast" of the show was made up of Cabaret Voltaire artists. Eggling appeared first, delivering a deadpan-serious speech about abstract art; in this context, it came across as a lampooning of abstraction, in some sense comparable to the cardboard-based mini-exhibition perched atop Farmer's dummy. Walter Serner later came to the stage dressed as a groom at a wedding, carrying a headless tailor's dummy. He offered a smell of artificial flowers to the dummy, and then laid the bouquet at its feet.

12 For discussion of theatrical aspects and the notions of staging and performance potential in Farmer's work, see Vanessa Desclaux, " 'To fabulate is to fabricate giants'," in *Geoffrey Farmer: Forgetting Air* (Rotterdam: Witte de With, 2008), 17–25; and Jessica Morgan, "Definition of a Farmer," in *Geoffrey Farmer* (Montreal: Musée d'art contemporain de Montréal, 2008), 95–98.

13 See Agnes Heller, "Five Approaches to the Phenomenon of Shame," *Social Research* 70, no. 4 (Winter 2003): 1015–30.

14 For another reading of this work, along with illuminating comments on the notions of authorship, process, and becoming in relation to Farmer's project, see Pierre Landry, "Where's Geoffrey," in Landry, ed., *Geoffrey Farmer* (Montreal: Musée d'art contemporain de Montréal, 2008), 89–93.

15 For a perceptive discussion of theatrical aspects of Farmer's project, with relevant comparison to William Leavitt's 1977 work *Spectral Analysis*, see Aram Moshayedi, "Sometimes There Is Trouble," in Heike Munder, et al., eds., *Geoffrey Farmer: Let's Make the Water Turn Black* (Zurich: Migros Museum für Gegenwartskunst and JRP Ringier, 2013), 80–82. In particular, Moshayedi discusses the notion of a "sculpture play" in relation to Farmer's project *Let's Make the Water Turn Black*, a work containing characters with seemingly self-evident names ("The Archer," "The Snuffleupagus," etc.).

16 See Rancière, *The Emancipated Spectator* (2008), trans. Gregory Elliott (London: Verso, 2009), 6–17.

17 For relevant discussion, see H. Porter Abbott, "Late Modernism: Samuel Beckett and the Art of the Oeuvre," in Enoch Brater and Ruby Cohn, eds., *Around the Absurd: Essays on Modern and Postmodern Drama* (Ann Arbor: University of Michigan Press, 1990), 73–96.

18 The provocative prominence assigned to details such as the tape clumps, front and center on the gallery stage, is analogous to Harold Pinter's unorthodox use of punctuation and pauses in ways that do not serve character development or plot advancement in the conventional sense. Known for the infamous "Pinter pause," he often presented subtly elliptical dialogue. Frequently, the primary things characters would address are replaced by ellipsis or dashes. The following exchange between Aston and Davies in *The Caretaker* is typical of Pinter, and seems somehow relevant to Farmer's personages:

ASTON. More or less exactly what you ...
DAVIES. That's it ... that's what I'm getting at is ... I mean, what sort of jobs ... (Pause.)

ASTON. Well, there's things like the stairs ... and the ... the bells ...
DAVIES. But it'd be a matter ... wouldn't it ... it'd be a matter of a broom
... isn't it?

19 The greatest satirists historically were capable of parodying and replicating
    others, setting aside and staging cultural fragments. We are coerced into
    beholding a hair or grub in amber; we gape at the insect and admire its
    fabulous urn, but wonder how the devil it got there. See Alexander Pope,
    "Epistle to Dr. Arbuthnot," in John Butt, ed., *The Poems of Alexander Pope*
    (New Haven: Yale University Press, 1963), 169–72. For helpful comments,
    see John R. Clark, "Vapid Voices and Sleazy Styles," in Brian A. Connery
    and Kirk Combe, eds., *Theorizing Satire: Essays in Literary Criticism*
    (New York: St. Martin's Press, 1995), 19–42.
20 See Barthes, "The Reality Effect" (1968), in Tzvetan Todorov, ed., *French
    Literary Theory Today* (New York and Paris: Cambridge University Press
    and Maison des Sciences de l'Homme, 1982), 11–17. See also Flaubert, *Un
    Coeur Simple*, in *Trois Contes* (Paris: Charpentier-Fasquelle, 1893), 4.
21 See Barthes, "The Reality Effect," 14.
22 For further discussion of this work, and insightful comments on Farmer's
    relationship to a diverse range of influences and sources—including Kathy
    Acker, Robert Filliou, and Mikhail Bakhtin—see Scott Watson, "Ghost/
    Face: Geoffrey Farmer," in *Geoffrey Farmer* (Montreal: Musée d'art
    contemporain de Montréal, 2008), 99–105.
23 I am reminded of an early Dada performance held in February of 1916
    at Cabaret Voltaire, in which a nineteen-year-old, monocle-wearing Tristan
    Tzara entered the stage singing sentimental melodies, and proceeded to
    hand out worthless wads of paper to scandalized spectators. Later on,
    Tzara left the stage to allow room for masked actors to prance around on
    stilts—gestures intended to frustrate seekers of any semblance of coherent
    narrative.
24 The terms of my discussion draw upon Martin Esslin's definition of the
    "theatre of the absurd." Esslin's is still one of the best sources on the subject.
    See Esslin, *The Theatre of the Absurd* (1961) (New York: Vintage, 2004).
25 One good, recent resource on Arte Povera is Carolyn Christov-Bakargiev,
    ed., *Arte Povera* (London: Phaidon, 1999), which contains texts by Celant
    and Grotowski, among others. For perceptive comments on the movement
    and its relationship to theatre, see Claire Gilman, "Pistoletto's Staged
    Subjects," *October* 124 (Spring 2008): 53–74, and Rosalind E. Krauss,
    "Giovanni Anselmo: Matter and Monochrome," *October* 124 (Spring
    2008): 125–36.
26 See Verwoert, "The Devils Inside the Thing Speak to the Devils Outside," in
    Eva Grubinger and Jörg Heiser, eds., *Sculpture Unlimited* (Berlin: Sternberg
    Press, 2011), 82–97. For further discussion of the notions of animism and
    materialism in Farmer's recent work, see Verwoert, "Coming to Life," *Frieze*
    147 (May 2012): 151–57.
27 See Verwoert, "The Devils Inside the Thing Speak to the Devils
    Outside," 87.

28 See McMullan, *Performing Embodiment in Samuel Beckett's Drama* (New York: Routledge, 2010), 110.

29 In some cases, like Krapp's tape recorder, objects become a substitute for an absent human Other. In *Rockaby*, W resorts to the rocking chair, which becomes expressive of a non-psychologized being. In such situations, often a kind of transference takes place back and forth between bodies and objects, contributing to a character's taking on a provisional status, on a non-verbal level, as atmosphere rather than as a person-product with clearly defined boundaries.

30 See Eyal Chowers, *The Modern Self in the Labyrinth: Politics and the Entrapment Imagination* (Cambridge, MA: Harvard University Press, 2004), esp. 109.

4   Liz Magor
"The Mouth and Other Storage Facilities"

Liz Magor's exhibition "The Mouth and Other Storage Facilities" starts with a stag's head.[1] Residing on a shelf—fastened to long, slender metal poles extending from floor to ceiling—the deer is illuminated by a halogen fixture, possibly lifted from an architect's drafting desk. But the way this creature is staged and situated implies a reverence that suggests museum and high-end retail environments. I momentarily consider cultures of the hunting trophy, in the home or clubhouse, and yet this unlucky specimen is cut too high on the neck and looks rather young and diminutive to serve the demands of machismo. He is rendered in white, with illusionistic details extending to an unevenness of cartilage in the ears and bumps at the bases of the antlers. The high degree of verisimilitude is made stranger by the surprise of real hairs creeping out from the sculptural material (a polymerized gypsum). My abrupt realization that I am looking at a cast of the dead is tempered by art-historical associations with the painterly tradition of studying animal corpses. But the unnatural blankness of the head, and the absence of other connections to still-life convention, serves to broaden and diversify his semiotic resonance. Coldly lit surfaces bring to mind marble statues of the decapitated John the Baptist. And another aspect adds to this anthropomorphizing: before being cast, woven material was inserted into the animal's neck, and this protrudes in a way that recalls the seductive folds of drapery adorning Pieta statues.[2]

Indeed, *Bedside* (2007) wavers between domestic, institutional, and commercial contexts of display. Here, the terms of *tainted goods* operate through the juxtaposition of textiles, animals, consumer products, and other household items in a manner that functions allegorically. I wish to confront, circulate, and consider them in ways that generate insights about identity, by failing to overcome the distance between signifier and signified, a gap that is overshadowed by an absence—of literal human characters with which I might identify and consume with ease.[3] While wandering about Magor's installation in Seattle—populated mostly by cast objects positioned in clusters on long tables with cast tops—one

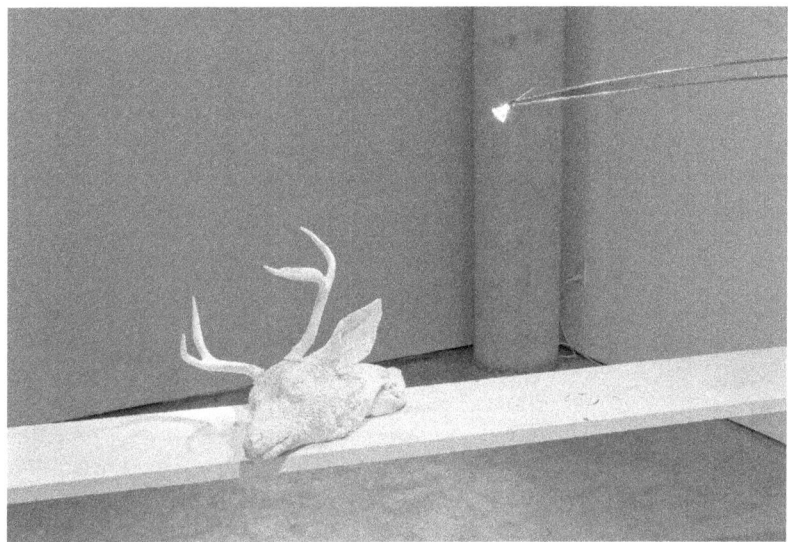

Figure 4.1 Liz Magor, *Bedside*, 2007
Polymerized gypsum, hardware, lighting fixture 109 × 17 × 73 in. (305 × 244 × 46 cm)
Installation view, "The Mouth and Other Storage Facilities," Henry Art Gallery, Seattle, WA, 2008
Photo: SITE Photography. Courtesy of Catriona Jeffries, Vancouver

experienced a series of discontinuities, triggering speculation about how people are compelled to abstract from the idea of the individualized and centered self, while categorizing others and constructing difference.

A sense of disjunction is felt frequently when turning away from the stag's head to confront the bulk of Magor's installation which, at first glance, resembles the aftermath of a festive event. The party's skeletal structure appears to have survived, as a group of sturdy tables, arranged in a manner that simultaneously suggests a buffet venue and retail environment, inviting both sweeping perusals and minute inspections of displayed items, including run-of-the-mill fare and a smorgasbord of curiosities: serving trays, clothing, liquor bottles, candy wrappers, chunks of bread, plastic-wrapped boxes of cigarettes, cigarette butts, sticks of gum, a raccoon, a mouse, a bird, squirrels, and much more. Magor serves up this motley cast of materials with varying degrees of mimetic fidelity to the real. Despite their wide-ranging presentation and the impressive intricacies of their depiction, the objects themselves—unlike those rendered in similarly sprawling banquet table scenes by

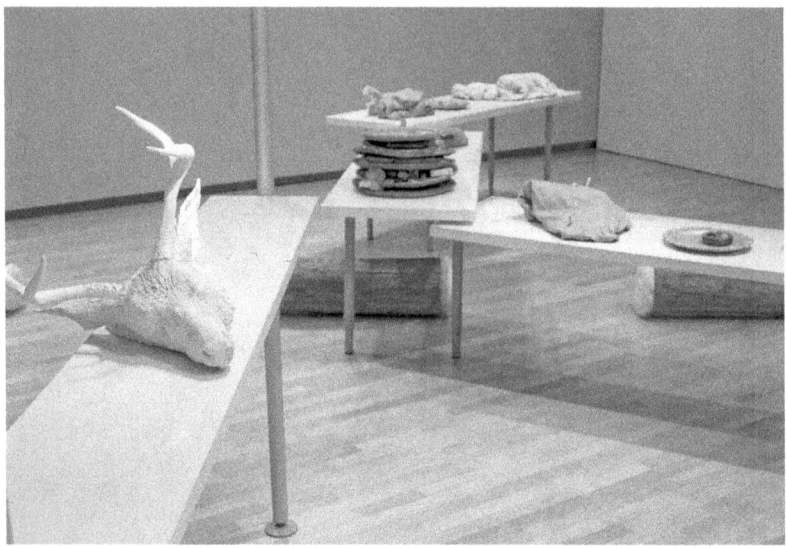

Figure 4.2 Liz Magor, Installation view, "The Mouth and Other Storage Facilities," Henry Art Gallery, Seattle, WA, 2008
Photo: SITE Photography. Courtesy of Catriona Jeffries, Vancouver

historical still-life painters—do not register as highly sought-after items or as singular signs of elevated social status. They are, for the most part, humble. Rather than luxury and abundance, many of these items signify processes of depletion and the consequences of consumption. Magor's material exhibits careful and respectful handling, but there are plenty of indications of abuse, disregard, and violence: the remains of sweets and other foodstuffs are frequently placed on platters, perhaps by a proprietor who was unconcerned with clearing them off. Despite being petrified in white plaster, imprinted and captured as sculptural units for posterity, these things may present a decomposing condition.

But Magor's compositional cocktail is conceptually more multifaceted than that. Sensing that something else is afoot, I survey Magor's cast of characters in detail. Placed at the end of one tabletop, *Tweed (Toblerone)* (2008) represents a wool coat that was, before casting, loosely folded with some reverence, perhaps as though the wearer were recently deceased. A sense of prolonged use is felt in the well-worn texture and in the muted tones of the collar and shoulder areas. Protruding from the garment is the box of an actual Toblerone chocolate bar— suggesting that a hole was cut into the plaster before insertion—with its three-sided tubular shape, well known to consumers. Placed on other

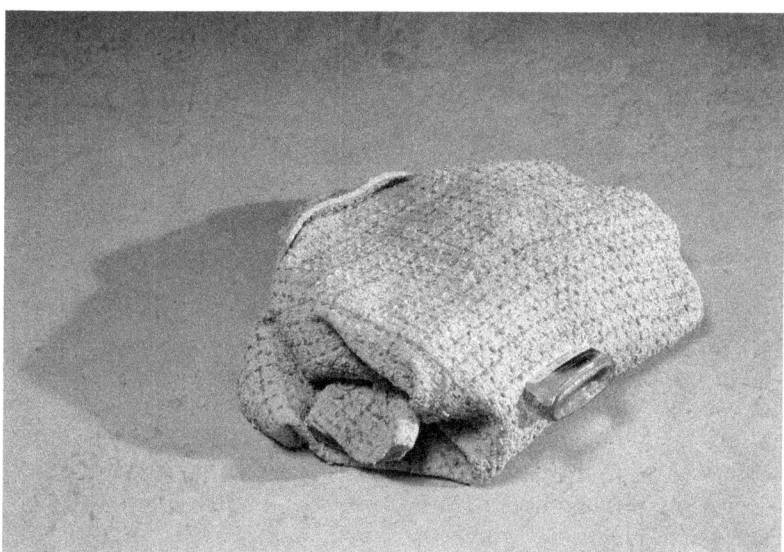

Figure 4.3 Liz Magor, *Tweed (Kidney)*, 2008
Polymerized gypsum, found object, 6 × 18 × 17 in. (15 × 46 × 43 cm)
Installation view, "The Mouth and Other Storage Facilities," Henry Art Gallery, Seattle, WA, 2008
Photo: SITE Photography. Courtesy of Catriona Jeffries, Vancouver

tables are *Tweed (Kidney)* and *Tweed (Neck)* (both from 2008). These works have bottles of whiskey, similarly deposited into cast wool articles of outerwear. One of these has red and wine strands of material, while the other combines a beige background color with more fragmentary green, red, and blue smudges, smears, and spots. On a technical level, I first wonder just how this cast clothing's colors had been rendered, and then consider the surface as an abstract pigmented pattern, resistant, in its plaster, table-based objecthood, to being received as a painting on (woven) canvas that maybe was meant to be hung on the wall. Despite the staying power implied by gypsum, Magor's introduction of pro- truding, "real" consumer products—some with limited shelf lives, like chocolate—contributes to a sense of a tension with traditional notions of precious, fine-art products.

The titular terms "kidney" and "neck" draw attention to where the bottles have been surgically implanted, hence enhancing a morbid mood of bodily awareness: a linguistic prodding to imagine the jacket being worn to the point of permanently imprinting a wearer's physique, or perhaps to the point of becoming a booze-infused cadaver. In the case of *Tweed (Neck)*, the bottle—still filled with amber liquid—has indeed been positioned where the neck of the wearer would be, thus establishing a connection between bottle and a vulnerable spot, located between mind and body, suggesting the dictum: "We are what we drink." Feeding an addiction, a body may become like a plaster shell, lacking any depth of personality. This may be signified by how others are labeled (e.g., as a "substance abuser") or by oneself, perpetually in pursuit of the next fix.[4] Ultimately, self-recognition may no longer be possible, as one becomes an Other to strangers and loved ones, a mere plaster shell.

Up close and personal, these plaster portrayals of painted wool—abruptly wedded to glass bottles—Magor's display recalls Raphaelle Peale's pictures from the early 1820s, showing things with an unusual intimacy, an over-descriptive intensity. Peale portrays friendly, benign objects that exude a sense of safety and playfulness, but these are juxtaposed with depictions of meat and split-open melons with anatomical implications, which come across as chilly and anxiety-inducing. Peale's tireless effort to capture close-up realities—such as the material densities and skins of mere berries—is a descriptive feat that carries weight partially because of how it indirectly incorporates an activity of bodily projection. When representing distant objects, it is easier to create the illusion of a disembodied vision—losing track of one's own body as orienting the spectacle—so that it may seem a purely mindful projection. But Magor and Peale render things at hand in a markedly more palpable and phenomenological fashion. These renderings cannot quite become "objects" existing apart from our material selves; they are somehow intertwined with, and complicated by, the bodies of beholders.[5] Indeed, Magor's display refuses a clear-cut separation of subject and object, wavering between the condition of "imperious conceptualizer and a desensualized world of things-become-concepts."[6] A foreign object (a bottle, a candy bar) abruptly breaks the seamless and smooth contours of a subject—so sensitively and splendidly described—implying a selfhood that is no longer secure, that is compromised.

In this sense, Magor's use of clothing is reminiscent of Robert Rauschenberg's integration of textiles into early Combines such as *Charlene* (1954). Within a relatively complex compositional field, a sweatshirt figures prominently; he stretched it, skin-like, across a panel, with paint stains and splatters situated so that they may serve as subtle signs for the body's libidinal and pulsating processes. As Graham Bader has observed, the uncertainty that is central to the understanding of his work uneasily combines material experience *and* the concept of confronting another body. Following the structure of assemblage, both Magor and Rauschenberg explore the body's dual status as both carnal substance (a site of desire, potentially to be penetrated) and signifying

surface (a site to be labelled and explained): as subjects to be touched
and texts to be read. As Bader notes, relevant in this regard is Jean-
François Lyotard's notion of "Moebian skin" with surfaces made up of
multiple textures, covered in corners, creases, and cavities. For Lyotard,
such skin lies beyond a Freudian schema rooted in a rigid division
between exterior and interior—and beyond a Lacanian framework that
understands desire as deriving solely from a condition of lack. Rather,
such a skin is the body, "open and spread ... as if your dressmaker's
scissors were opening the leg of an old pair of trousers."[7] Accordingly,
I choose not to reductively read Magor's project solely in terms of an
iconography of loss. Her display is also hopeful and generative, a stage
set populated by unexpected bodies and unlikely characters, with just
the right amount of fragmentary features to provoke mobile musing
about what or who is on hand.

Rather than alcohol, it is nicotine that flavors the character and cor-
puses of *Leather (1 Cig)*, *Leather (4 Cigs)*, and *Leather (Ashtray)* (all
from 2008). Juxtaposed with cigarettes and ashes, jackets have been
gathered up and folded so that they seem ready for storage or packing
in luggage. These non-trendy textiles have been "cast" to play the role of
receptacle, not for a human body but for cigarettes. I read these re-casted
materials—the jacket becomes an ashtray—as productively opaque, partially freed from instrumentalized forms of communicative meaning. At
first, they may register as animal-skinned beings subject to acts of violence
or violation. *Leather (1 Cig)* features a faded yellow (nicotine-stained)
cast coat, with done-up buttons, containing a gray sweater—a quality
comparable to the drapery stuffed into the stag's neck—which/who has
been stuck with a single cigarette, perhaps one burning at the moment of
insertion. Further, one might associate the combined activities of casting
and penetration by a tobacco product and a phallic form with the construction of difference. This leather-clad creature could be summarily
dismissed or denigrated as a "smoker." And these smoky semantics shift
by increasing the number of inserted cigarettes, as in *Leather (4 Cig)*, in
which a gray garment is penetrated four times, thereby connoting, but
never declaring, sacrificial images of St. Sebastian. A further move—
from the solemnity of Christian iconography to the profanity of the rude
abuser—occurs with *Leather (Ashtray)*, in which a similar expanse of
animal hide is cast and subjected to an irreverent scattering of ash, perhaps the result of a bullying cigarette flick, a gesture not causing physical pain (or death), but intended to insult. It is the absence of human
wearers for such plaster renderings, combined with the recognition of the
contrasting presence of actual cigarettes, which provokes such readings,
subjective as they are.

And yet, I then move from contexts of death and disparagement
to the idea that these *Leather* figures may be reverent offerings that

are intended to express, or somehow embody, vows. Traditionally, ex-votos are images or objects displayed in thanks for an answered prayer. Sometimes sculptural depictions of ailing body parts that had been healed, votive offerings may signify proof of divine favor or may serve as testaments of renewed faith following a prolonged ordeal. In the case of Magor's jacket-based works, the nature of such ailments remains nebulous. However they do encourage speculation about preparatory rites, painstakingly performed and identified with the portrayal of a person who has been under duress for a prolonged period of time, perhaps falling prey to a damaging desire—for smokes, for booze, or for relief and resolution, from an identity or a body that is forever in flux. In their fragmented referencing of organs and skins, Magor's votives may reflect a performative process of freeing the self, from a state that is fractured. And her work may be meant to reflect the remnants of such repeated rituals—of casting, of juxtaposition, of incantation—that were successful. Like a jacket, the disease or the damaging desire could, maybe for a moment, have been shed.

Georges Didi-Huberman has discussed a vast collection of ex-votos found in Exeter Cathedral in 1943.[8] Arranged in the vicinity of a bishop's tomb, they included small-scale figurines, anatomical fragments, and masses of raw and non-figurative wax. In the case of the body parts, a site of suffering is represented. But the unworked wax offerings were each regarded as deeply and intimately meaningful; despite the abstraction, they were in keeping with a notion of secret signification identified with a single person, an incarnation of one self. Such reductive renderings lie at the other end of the representational spectrum from portrait busts that serve up detailed descriptions of a character as an easy-to-consume, coherent whole. For Didi-Huberman, wax was a preferred material partly because of its malleability and transformability, identified with a belief in imitative magic and in the idea of "psychic temporal gain." This material allows for a temporal extension from the moment when the vow is made: "[A]dapting itself plastically to misfortunes and to prayers, it can change when symptoms and desires change."[9] Wax permits the gain of flesh, registering as a material of desire—a life conferred on it by the simple warmth of hands. Relevant to Magor's practice is the idea of "ascetic" humility identified with non-portraiture and the rendering of plaster with broader bodily significance. For Magor, the votive may also take the form of a vow and a highly personal desire that is rooted in the vulnerable and visceral aspects of the votive scenario: my suffering organ, my clothes, etc. Her "offerings" give form to psychic time, and could signify a sudden change from misfortune into miracle. In the gallery, the viewer may envision tables inhabited by relics giving thanks for this relief, reverently lit artifacts that emanate in the wake of a psychically processed ordeal. They may be objects of psychic significance, supported by the ways in which they are given. In devoting them—after casting and combining them with other things—the giver indicates that he or she holds them dear, or is beholden to them. Crucially, such offerings need not be precious or valuable commodities in the conventional sense: a single article of clothing, a piece of cake, an animal, and so on.

Even Magor's tabletops—also cast in gypsum and combined with consumable goods—reflect these tensions of mind and body, between offence and offerings, between allegorical allusions to destructive behaviors and to hopeful relationships of reverence and respect. Supported by found legs—deriving from worktables—these five rectilinear objects (all from 2008) shift between the status of mere support surfaces and of altars for enacting rites. While some have empty objects (an ashtray, a candy wrapper) embedded in their plaster flesh, all of them are infused with stains and smudges that may indicate either a repeated practice of sacrifice or a compulsive consumption of goods that are not good for me. But combined with these features are cracks and fissures in this pseudo-furniture which are tainted, in their unexpected ability to reflect bodily processes and fluids, and to serve as signs ranging from the reckless and libidinal to the intellectualized and careful, from the base to the spiritual, from the profane to the sacred to the utterly mundane. Hence, while inspecting their surfaces and textures, these tops become surprising symbols for a self that is fractured and fragmentary, yet continually striving for something (or someone) further. Such tensions are, in some sense, reminiscent of Robert Gober's renderings of doors or sinks, representing states of reverence and reproach, love and hate.[10] There are layered associations with a body consumed, wasted, or burned out—or honored and cleansed. And Gober does similarly identify with contexts of altar and slaughterbench, remembrance and oblivion, devotion and destruction, albeit in a manner more rooted in a specific (Catholic) sense of spiritual conflict.[11]

Elsewhere in the table-based installation, Magor throws animals into the mix, creatures that enact—with theatrical flavors of immediacy and intimacy—semantic shifts between the status of human, animal, and lifeless object.[12] The cast of a raccoon lies prominently on one table. It has been captured in a curled-up position akin to sleep, but the assertive and regular alignment of limbs—with head, hands, feet, and tail all meeting in close proximity—suggest human intervention, and a similar sense of ritualistic manipulation. Paws are neatly and respectfully placed atop one another. Perhaps he or she died happy, while imbibing and scavenging party leftovers. Or he/she may have been poisoned, and later reverently prepared for the afterlife by someone sympathetic. But *Raccoon* (2008) is of course an assemblage, also featuring a tray, candies, and a bowl, all of which rest on a cast piece of fabric. The curvatures

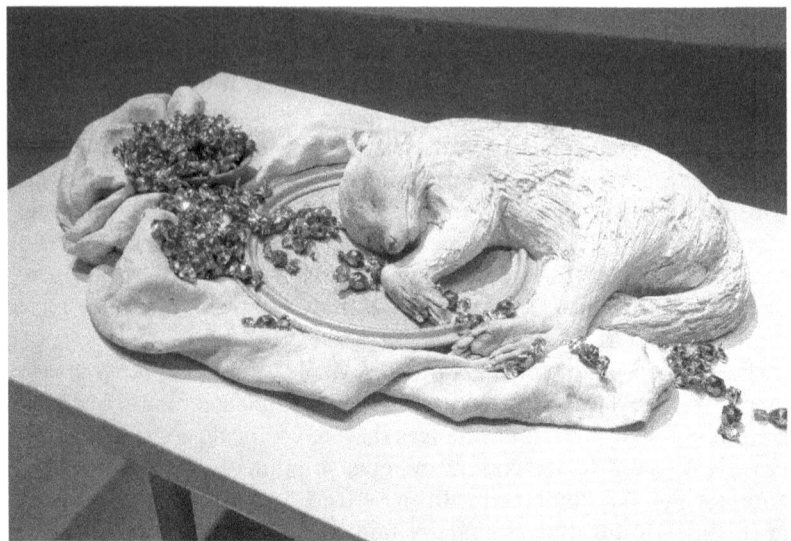

Figure 4.4 Liz Magor, *Raccoon*, 2008
Polymerized gypsum, candies, 5 × 21 × 33 in. (13 × 54 × 83 cm)
Installation view, "The Mouth and Other Storage Facilities," Henry Art Gallery, Seattle, WA, 2008
Photo: SITE Photography. Courtesy of Catriona Jeffries, Vancouver

of the raccoon's back and head carefully echo those of the tray. As with *Bedside*, individual hairs may be discerned, poking through the plaster surface.[13] But compared to the cast stag, here there are more generalized expanses of fur that are painterly in texture. The white and abstracted areas of the raccoon's torso and back contrast with extremities—the snout, the tip of the tail, the individual pads on each paw—rendered in minute detail, with charcoal accents. And yet almost all of it registers within a monochrome context, from white to gray. The restricted color range may be read in terms of a leveling activity associated with casting—as a process of reproduction, made all the more apparent by being juxtaposed with gleaming and non-cast blue-and-silver candies, scattered near the head and placed in the bowl.

Magor's process is one that integrates intricate imprinting and manipulating activities—and may be intended to reanimate bodies, both human and non-human. Such activity may be read in relation to rituals meant to invoke the supernatural realm. It is conventionally the case today that we converse with images and things (i.e., screens) as though they were living bodies, and to accept them in place of actual bodies. To some extent, such customs originate with archaic societies' association of images with those no longer in the land of the living, no longer present in their bodies, or those that remain in a state of limbo.[14] Some cultic communities felt the need to consecrate or anoint certain objects—such as animals, food, or everyday articles, like trays and clothing, identified with the departed—so as to reanimate them: these items were composed by an artisan but consecrated by a priest or shaman, who converted the things in question into a medium, with the power to transmit images from beyond.

However, Magor's *Raccoon* may also be a rendering of rest. It may be read as part of a materialist strategy of facilitating contemplative resistance—to oppressive economic and cultural imperatives which are increasingly against all kinds of repose, particularly those divorced from digital networks. As Jonathan Crary has argued, slumber these days has become "… a figure for a subjectivity on which power can operate with the least political resistance *and* a condition that finally cannot be instrumentalized or controlled externally—that evades or frustrates the demands of global consumer society."[15] Situated in states of semi- or unconsciousness, Magor's animals represent a wavering condition, between vulnerability and trust, between exposure and care. They allude to the relation between the safekeeping of others and the revivifying carelessness which prolonged periods of rest and sleep can provide. Crary's polemic against regimes of digital personalization and self-administration is one worth recognizing in relation to Magor's sculptural statements:

> Any apparent technological novelty is also a qualitative dilation of one's accommodation to and dependence on 24/7 routines; it is also part of an expansion in the number of points at which an individual is made into an application of new control systems and enterprises.[16]

Strewn next to the snoozing raccoon are vibrant and shiny candies, which may signify this realm of restless, immaterial consumption and circulation—one with empty calories, as it were—that depends on the accelerating pace of novelty production, and a corresponding disablement of collective memory and historical awareness. Increasingly, we live in a world engaged in the ongoing management of attentiveness and the impairment of perception within compulsory routines. Crary notes that committing to activities where time spent cannot be leveraged through an interface, and its links, is now something to be avoided or done sparingly. As with the experience economy discussed in my introductory chapter, the "24/7" world requires a strategic maintenance of the illusion of choice and autonomy, one of the foundations of a global system of auto-regulation.[17] Current media products are resources to be actively managed and manipulated, exchanged, reviewed, archived, recommended, or "followed." Any act of viewing is layered with options for simultaneous and interruptive actions, choices, and feedback. The system depends on normalizing the idea of a continuous interface—one that aspires to be seamless in its engagement with illuminated screens that unremittingly demand interest or response. Incorporating figures of rest and repose in which decelerated and manual manipulation has undoubtedly played a role—and yet always complicated by found and cheap objects—Magor's display critiques the very notion of "saying" anything with speed, or with communicative clarity and efficiency, including marketing messages. She sets a stage upon which one stands a chance to stake a speculative claim within such hegemonic environments of acceleration. Her assemblage-based scenario offers the opportunity to carve out singular temporalities and durations which—partly due to their slowness—are partially resistant to systems and economies of control which depend on rapid speeds of processing. Against this backdrop, the physical circulation around her sculptural setting may become a restorative withdrawal, signifying a set of speculative habits and gestures that is intrinsically incompatible with the current capitalist marketplace—which now operates through every hour of the day and night, pushing us into constant activity, eroding forms of community, historical memory, and political expression.

And it is such staged deterioration in Magor's work that spurs me to speculate about Samuel Beckett's plays. As Stan Gontarski has argued, Beckett's late work in particular is "an art of icons, images, and afterimages, ghosts of memories," that is "as closely related to sculpture as to what we have traditionally called theatre."[18] *Krapp's Last Tape* (1958), for example, is about a 69-year-old man's failing memories of his younger self, supplemented by audio recordings heard on a reel-to-reel tape player. Krapp is presented as barely more alive than the documents that surround him, arranged as an "archival" collection of boxes and spools that register, along with his body, as the objectified and shameful result of a dysfunctional life. Here technology cannot provide redemption or renewal, endlessly repeating Krapp's destitution and with it a growing sense of amnesia, as he is unable to remember some of the decaying recordings that he consults. The absurdist role of repetition in Beckett is crucial to consider in terms of a "groaning thematics of memory," identified with recordings that can no longer serve their informational purpose efficiently: the audience is able to share in the dramatization of forgetting, shame, and loss on the level of a not-so-living monument. To remember (or memorialize) Krapp is to participate in shared amnesia. Indeed, according to Pierre Nora, "we share so much of memory because there is so little of it left."[19] For Nora, the archive has become the deliberate and calculated secretion of lost memory. It adds life to itself—often a function of its own recording—"a second memory, a prosthesis-memory". Our cultural moment is that of the immanent disappearance of an "immense and intimate fund of memory," leaving behind only "a reconstituted object beneath the gaze of critical history."

Squirrel (Cake) (2008) features a similar juxtaposition of animal, serving platter, packaging, and candy—in this case actual chocolate bonbons, wrapped in gold and red foil and inserted directly into the surrounding table. As with *Raccoon*, the palette is muted, mostly dark and silvery grays, except for a piece of off-white cake with gray and brown details signifying mold. Again, the squirrel's body follows the curve of the tray, suggesting preparatory rites, performed prior to receiving a mummifying mask. It is worthwhile to reflect on the reverent connotation of this care, operating in tension with a notion of disparagement associated with a pest (squirrel) and the impermanency implied by the valueless materials (aged cake) awaiting disposal.

But one is struck by the hyperrealism of isolated details, especially the claws and mouth, tinged with actual brown hairs. Magor's casting method is indeed mimetically powerful, but only in a selective sense. She shows some of the animal's individualized characteristics—only sometimes revealing what makes a squirrel a squirrel or maybe what makes *this* squirrel unique. It is this aspect—along with Magor's commitment to the chromatic context of historical photography—which allows her project to be best read as an allegorical reflection on how and why we categorize, regulate, and control human beings. Relevant in this regard is Allan Sekula's classic commentary on photography's nineteenth-century development, in terms of tensions between the need for fulfillment of a bourgeois notion of the self and the need to establish and delimit the terrain of the Other. Photography has formed part of a regulatory practice, performed and displayed in institutions ranging from the asylum to the museum to the factory employment office, sites in which supposedly objective means are used to record and label the suspect, the deviant, and the biologically inferior—those deserving of shame.[20] In addition, Magor compositionally sandwiches together the animal with food and other table-based motifs as a means to address the human body's relationship to the concepts of appetite and hygiene, notions that relate to basic levels of existence and survival. As Norman Bryson has noted, the display of animals within a table setting has historically signified criticism of the lower-classes that, like animals, have been associated with moral insensitivity, irrationality, and the lower functions of the body (consumption, procreation, ingestion).[21] Squirrels and raccoons have, in fact, traditionally been consumed in North America by rural communities, but are frequently regarded elsewhere as pests, as those that

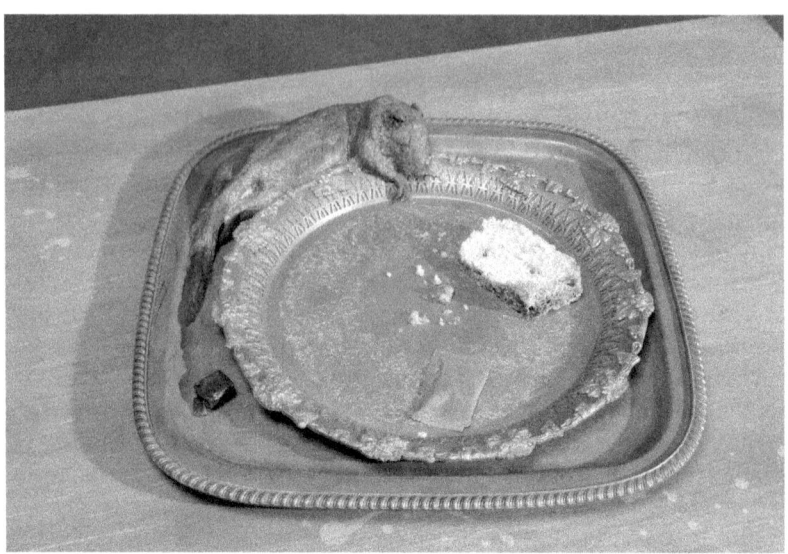

Figure 4.5 Liz Magor, *Squirrel (Cake)*, 2008
Polymerized gypsum, 5 × 24 × 31 in. (13 × 60 × 80 cm)
Installation view, "The Mouth and Other Storage Facilities," Henry Art Gallery, Seattle, WA, 2008
Photo: SITE Photography. Courtesy of Catriona Jeffries, Vancouver

scavenge on waste or swipe food (from gardens) according to relentless, uncivilized instincts to survive and thrive.

By fully falling prey to compulsive, self-destructive, or unhealthy behaviors and desires—not just for another shot of sugar, booze, or nicotine—people may qualify themselves for social regulation, according to the societal compulsion to exercise the dictates of difference, the designation of the abnormal. They qualify because "they" are envisioned as letting go of their analytical minds to the extent that they are now subject to control from without. Many such cultures of control have nineteenth-century origins, and coincide with the development of photographic technologies. These technologies—which in some sense are comparable to Magor's casting technique—were initially associated by their inventors with miraculous phenomena. Henry Fox Talbot's camera-less method of photographic contact printing was regarded as a process of exact, indexical copying of intricate details (of, say, a jacket or a decorative tray) and the implosion of representation and reality (culture and nature) that the medium allowed.

Still-life's early seventeenth-century Dutch inception occupied the lowest position in the hierarchy of artistic genres, with its preoccupation with objects that formerly had existed on the margins of religious scenes. Mere props, so to speak. Bryson addresses a culture of the table that became serially represented in these pictures. The repetitious representation of mundane material—comparable to the trays and foodstuffs in Magor's work—generated a discourse with temporal qualities distinct from histories occupied by heroic personages and events of consequence: "Besides the rapid, seismically sensitive rhythms set by consumption, [still-life] objects are also tuned to a slow, almost geological, rhythm that is all their own."[22] Magor expresses this table-based rhythm—rooted in the basic acts of drinking, snacking, and smoking— identified intuitively with a realm of routine in which the monumental or momentous is not expected. This normally is a stage upon which forgettable actions are performed, frequently to ensure survival, socialization, and self-maintenance.

Magor's still-life scenario has human agency and time flowing through them. Indeed, the rendering of gypsum reflects—in ways that, needless to say, differ fundamentally from paint—the practice of smoothing them and tending to them through countless acts of handling and attention. The result is a beholding experience identified with the "steadying hand of cultural memory" and an accompanying sense of generational continuity, portrayed long ago by George Kubler according to his theory of "prime objects." In Magor's display, one may discern a distillation of ritualized memory that is melded to "characters" of the kind that do not cohere into packaged protagonists driving a plot.[23] Forms of table and tray never need to be re-invented from scratch or thought-through from first principles every time they are needed. When encountering such items, the beholder subordinates the impulse of invention to the authority of cultural formulae. It follows that still life is capable of signifying the *potential* for expendability of individuals' creative, social, or cultural contributions.

Magor's table scene enacts a transition, away from a place of plentitude and spectacle associated with the feeding of specific egos. Much of these dining surfaces are populated by a mere smattering of depleted cigarettes and containers that are predominantly empty. The general absence of color further signifies that much of this spread yielded its oral pleasures long ago. Indeed, Magor crafts a singular temporality tied to a sculptural critique of moralizing still-life traditions, centered on themes of excess. With *Tray (Bird/Heart)*, Magor displays real gold-foil-wrapped chocolates, starkly apparent and gleaming within their cast heart-shaped container; these are situated next to the cast of a decomposed bird, itself a diminutive signifier of a flightless soul which, when juxtaposed with the seductive sweets, may be a sign for a culture of addiction, perhaps in terms of its human or physiological costs (given the cardiac reference provided by the candy box) or the consequences of empty calories (the obesity epidemic).[24] But given the addition of extinguished cigarettes, one may speculate about nicotine within a relatively benign context, as a substance that serves as regressive outlet for oral stimulation, a means to cope with anxiety or to suppress other libidinal appetites.

In considering these human costs, I recall Siegfried Kracauer's articles in the *Frankfurter Zeitung* from the 1920s and early 1930s that drew attention to problematic non-participants, inhabiting (or haunting) metropolitan spaces, who cannot engage in consumption in efficient, progressive, and current ways. These dysfunctional residents were labeled, homogenized, abstracted, and isolated as lacking in social capital. The employment office and daytime shelters were popularly described as alienating spaces that processed society's "waste products," and were often instructively referred to in contrast with those who visibly (and responsibly) are seen to consume along with associated sites of efficient production, circulation, and display of goods (offices and department stores). In the down-and-out places, for instance, there was an ostensible lack of reflective surfaces (after all, who would want to display his or her poverty to oneself or others?).[25] Kracauer further observed a tendency toward repeated conversations and an overriding concern with basic necessities, but also with "fetishized" objects (such as cigarettes) that "cease being merely wares and become irreplaceable goods ..." Such ostracized people repeatedly seek out assemblage-like conglomerations of tobacco, shoes, sweaters, coats, liquor, and other items that are deemed signs of pathological and compulsive behaviors (in contrast to progressive and self-fulfilling habits of fetishistic consumption). Occupants of these lowly spaces occupy a generalized waiting position—an "enforced idleness"—identified with abstract states of purposelessness, desperation, and aimlessness. "Waiting almost becomes an end in itself ... I know of no [other] type of place where waiting would be so demoralizing." Kracauer emphasizes an absence of specific personal or political meanings in these conversations, one among many signs of a predicament, in which people are caught up in the process of becoming comparable to defective products, within a space of "mass storage."

Magor's repeated placement of petrified animal imagery in such works ensures a morbid element which—in her case, is never is allowed to dominate—as a reminder of death or destructive lifestyles. As Hanneke Grootenboer has explored, vanitas images posit the ontological difference between being and nothingness, as well as the notion of the inevitability of death.[26] Vanitas messages have for centuries warned against the weakness of indulgence in earthly pleasures, with such statements frequently taking the form of spectacular displays of indulgence—as in the case of *tour de force* banquet scenes painted by Jan Davidsz. De Heem or Willem Kalf. But of greater relevance to Magor's project are still life pictures that offer more humble repasts. Pieter Claesz., for example, specialized in so-called breakfast paintings featuring just a few inconsequential motifs. Seemingly arbitrary and incidental, these objects were formulaically depicted by Claesz. on tables set against bare backgrounds. In a sense, Claesz.'s *Little Breakfast* (1636) features the afterlives of objects, symbols that have forgotten their previous appearances as sacred constructs situated on the margins of religious paintings; as marginal subjects, they never shed their status as an Other, as excessive pieces of information in works which, for Bryson, exceed the minimal schema needed to recognize the picture's essential story. And pictures such as *Little Breakfast* have a mostly monochromatic color scheme, which, significantly, was a feature first developed in land-scape paintings produced in response to changing market demands for mass-produced, less expensive works for a bourgeois audience. In this painting, the space is shallow, so that all objects appear within reach— a roll, a cracked nut, a sliced-up herring—with the knife and plate projecting outside of the frame, blurring the spatial division between viewer and picture in a theatrical manner that is, I would suggest, analo-gous to the experience of Magor's work.

The floor beneath Magor's tables is populated by six long objects resembling logs, arranged as a single straight line. Close inspection of surfaces—deep grooves, cracks, and heavily worn-down sections— does initially impress on the level of verisimilitude, a trompe l'oeil feat. This work, *Molly's Reach* (2005), may be associated with the activity of seeking out long-fallen trunks, each leading to a memorializing act of (arboreal) portraiture. The artist strove, perhaps, to emulate the tex-tural features that make each of these bodies a unique thing—carved, sectioned, eroded, and manipulated by the passage of time and weather, and maybe the more abrupt intervention (or execution) by an axe. These are not wooden originals, but have been cast with conscientious care, hollowed out and filled with foam, the flavor of which wavers from toxic industrial byproduct to benign, caramel-colored frothy filling. Once again, meticulously recorded surface details of bark operate in tension here with a non-mimetic and generalized color scheme. In this regard it is worth recalling Talbot's belief in the "pencil of nature," as a faith in a photographic process that is superhuman in its descriptive power. With a rigorously restricted palette, Magor's casting, like the camera, is a masterful means of capturing the minute details of natural phe-nomena, capable of producing documents that serve in the explanatory enterprise of categorizing specimens (botanical and human).[27]

The logs provide further fuel for slow-burning speculations about the practice and theory of mimesis within two- and three-dimensional contexts—logs and bark, sculpture and photography—and about how descriptive imaging functions in relation to structures of control or containment. The seductive perusing of Magor's bark terrain is complicated by the ways in which these log-like things are presented as a manufactured contrivance, as a stand-in for wood. Their entire surface has been uniformly rendered with a single shade of grayish brown, instilling a feeling of lifelessness suggesting the occurrence of petrification on forest floors. But in their pervasively regular muteness, they chromatically stray from that naturalistic context, opening them up to "unnatural" processes, such as the machinic activity of gutting logs for their pulp, an activity signified by the foam, which once was liquid and now here has hardened into a crust. Like much of Magor's installation, these objects may be read as imprints, as the death-masks of the leftovers or empty shells discarded by industry or consumers.

The industrial context of a mill is further referenced by a prevailing sense of compositional sameness. A straight-lined, non-hierarchical arrangement of cylindrical elements of roughly equal length and height, this line of overgrown pencils recall the serial logic of "one thing after another" espoused by minimalists such as Donald Judd who, in his more exactingly focused reverence for geometric expression, was disinterested in the hybridizing act of registering both machinic and natural phenomena. Consequently, the brand of sameness expressed in *Molly's Reach* better contributes to an aesthetic discourse about the consequences of the mechanization, depletion, and adaptation of nature. Such is a sampling of semantic roots that permit an envisioning of this wood-like, but not wooden, work—which, appropriately, underlies and bisects her whole show.

In terms of tainted goods, there is one further and crucial similarity between these loggy units and the tobacco- and booze-infused characters previously seen: they are all products, made possible by Magor's casting process and the inherent potential for production on an (pseudo)industrial scale. They are problematic products because they are drained of color and incorporate found articles, castaway stuff that do not at all seem novel, slick, or hip. Unwanted and unvalued, forest trash, cig butts, and worn-out textiles are staged so that they promote speculation about a loss of retail allure, or a shedding of the thin veneer of fashion. Her casting encourages the beholder to slow down, wander about, and listen to those neglected things, to understand their difference and their relationship to obsolescence—in ways that are analogous to the predicaments of people, or how they might struggle with desires, with compulsive and addictive behaviors, and with the ideas of value, relevance, and worth. In separate series of works—the Leathers, the Tweeds, the Tables—Magor employs repetition partly because she wishes to express the notion and ambition for mass production, while simultaneously suggesting compulsive and obsessive behaviors that may be unproductive and isolating. Indeed, Magor regularly mimics aspects of conventional manufacturing, but does so in ways that manually make room for unusual variations, oddities, and ambiguities, always courting with ideas of inefficiency—qualities that fail in the face of smoothly running, rapid, and relentless machines of marketing and manufacturing. While Magor's installation strikes some notes of optimistic production, it also conveys such failures—within displays that combine personalized "products" with signs of alienation and sedation.

Notes

1 Curated by Bill Jeffries and Sara Krajewski, the exhibition was held at the Henry Art Gallery, Seattle, and the Simon Fraser University Art Gallery, Vancouver, in 2008–09. My reading addresses a selective portion of the show.
2 For more discussion of *Bedside* and related works, see my review of Magor's exhibition at Susan Hobbs Gallery, Toronto, in *Artforum* (Summer 2007).
3 See Walter Benjamin, *The Origin of German Tragic Drama*, trans. J. Osbourne (London: Verso, 1998), 166, 184.
4 For some treatment of the theme of addiction in Magor's work, see Sara Krajewski, "Outside the Comfort Zone," in *Liz Magor: The Mouth and Other Storage Facilities* (Seattle and Vancouver: Henry Art Gallery and Simon Fraser University Gallery, 2008), 49–53.
5 See Maurice Merleau-Ponty, *Phenomenology of Perception* (1945), trans. Colin Smith (London: Routledge, 1996), 316–20.
6 As Alexander Nemerov has noted, "Without the tree's bark, the surface of the skin would itself be an abstraction. Without the density of specific things, the body's own thickness would become abstract." See Nemerov, *The Body of Raphaelle Peale: Still Life and Selfhood, 1812–1824* (Berkeley: University of California Press, 2001), 4–5, 31–32.
7 For excellent discussion, see Graham Bader, "Rauschenberg's Skin," *Grey Room* 27 (Spring 2007): 104–18. See Lyotard, *Libidinal Economy*, trans. Iain Hamilton Grant (Bloomington: Indiana University Press, 1974), 2–3.
8 See Didi-Huberman, "Ex-Voto: Image, Organ, Time," *L'Esprit Créateur*, 47, no. 3 (2007): 7–16, and idem, *Ex-voto: images, organe, temps* (Paris: Bayard, 2006). For some relevant comments on relationships between the ex-voto and conceptual art practices, see Irene V. Small, "Believing in Art: The Votive Structures of Conceptual Art," *RES: Anthropology and Aesthetics* 55/56 (Spring-Autumn 2009): 294–307.
9 Didi-Huberman, "Ex-Voto: Image, Organ, Time," 9.
10 Gober establishes an uncanny, symbolic continuum between domestic objects and the body in a manner that is relevant to Magor's practice as well. Freud was convinced that dream images of the house and its attributes (like staircases, windows, doors) represent, in veiled form, libidinal desires of an individual body. We may experience dread when confronting that which is "familiar and old-established in the mind [but] … has been estranged only by the process of repression." If survival of the "home"

as an institution for socialization depends on the repression of desire and fear, then memories of the home, when conjured involuntarily, may lead to uncanny sensations. See Freud, "The Uncanny" (1919), in *On Creativity and the Unconscious: Papers on the Psychology of Art, Literature, Love, Religion*, trans. A. Strachey (New York: Harper & Row, 1958). For some helpful commentary, see Nancy Spector, "Robert Gober: Homeward Bound/Auf der Heimreise," *Parkett* 27 (March 1991): 80–89.

11 For relevant discussion, see Hal Foster, "An Art of Missing Parts," *October* 92 (Spring 2000): 128–56. Of particular interest with regard to Magor's project are Foster's comments about Gober's method of "nursing" an image into material form. Of course, unlike Magor's assemblages, Gober's objects often look like readymades but they never are. But as with Magor's work, his readymade is represented but then suspended as a reference: "[A]uthorial origin is not flatly disavowed so much as slightly disturbed—just enough to be rendered enigmatic" (132). In this way of working, the artist does not so much invent forms "so much as retrace tableaux in which the subject is not fixed in relation to identity, difference, and sexuality ..." (134). The objects do seem at times to have arrived from another place, more unconscious than not, and hence encourage speculation. What does this Other want? What is a sexual object for me? Which gender or sexuality am I? In this regard, it is notable that Magor has exhibited with Gober several times.

12 These shifts are implied by the slide between animate and inanimate in the exhibition title "The Mouth and Other Storage Facilities."

13 Philp K. Dick's novel *Do Androids Dream of Electric Sheep?* (1968) is set in the near future, when live animals are rare commodities (compared to industrially produced ones, with programmed responses). Dick recounts the moment when the protagonist sees a live raccoon on display in the offices of a robotics corporation. The animal's astronomical cost becomes an overinvested sign mediating one's sense of wonderment and desire for something living and vulnerable like oneself.

14 For an intriguing discussion, see Hans Belting, "Image, Medium, Body: A New Approach to Iconology," *Critical Inquiry* 31 (Winter 2005): 302–19.

15 See Crary, *24/7: Late Capitalism and the Ends of Sleep* (London: Verso, 2013), 28.

16 Ibid., 43.

17 Ibid., 42, 56.

18 See S. E. Gontarski, "Reinventing Beckett," *Modern Drama* 49, no. 4 (Winter 2006): 428–51, 429.

19 See Nora, "Between Memory and History: Les Lieux de Mémoire," *Representations* 26 (1989): 7–24, 7, 14.

20 See Sekula, "The Traffic in Photographs," in Serge Guilbaut, et al., eds., *Modernism and Modernity: The Vancouver Conference Papers* (Halifax: Nova Scotia School of Art and Design Press, 1983), 121–54, 124. For relevant discussion of pictorial cultures that strive for an uncanny sense of equivalence between human and animal "portraits"—which may disrupt hierarchies of both natural and social order, see Alex Potts, "Natural Order and the Call

of the Wild: The Politics of Animal Picturing," *Oxford Art Journal* 13, no. 1 (1990): 12–33.

21 See Bryson, *Looking at the Overlooked: Four Essays on Still Life Painting* (Cambridge, MA: Harvard University Press, 1990). My discussion is also indebted to Hanneke Grootenboer's excellent study, *The Rhetoric of Perspective: Realism and Illusionism in Seventeenth-Century Dutch Still-Life Painting* (Chicago: University of Chicago Press, 2005).

22 See Bryson, *Looking at the Overlooked*, 13.

23 For discussion of Kubler, temporality, and conceptualism see Pamela M. Lee, *Chronophobia: On Time in the Art of the 1960s* (Cambridge, MA: MIT Press, 2006).

24 For insightful discussion of the role of irrationality, unhealthy food, and social class in Magor's work, see Reid Shier, "Crack in the Rock," in *Liz Magor* (Toronto and Vancouver: Art Gallery of York University and Contemporary Art Gallery, 2000), 82–84.

25 For discussion, see Henrik Reeh, *Ornaments of the Metropolis: Siegfried Kracauer and Modern Urban Culture* (1991), trans. John Irons (Cambridge, MA: MIT Press, 2004), 123–28, 131.

26 According to Christian doctrine, the moment of death is the instance when biographical time stops, and a transitory stage begins; this stage is on the way to the continuum of eternity where time does not exist. See Grootenboer, *The Rhetoric of Perspective: Realism and Illusionism in Seventeenth-Century Dutch Still-Life Painting* (Chicago: University of Chicago Press, 2005).

27 For a perceptive treatment of Talbot and positivist thought, see Carol Armstrong, *Scenes in a Library: Reading the Photograph in the Book, 1843–1875* (Cambridge, MA: MIT Press, 1998). For a discussion of otherness in Magor's log works, see Nancy Tousley, "Into the Woods," in *Liz Magor* (Toronto and Vancouver: Art Gallery of York University and Contemporary Art Gallery, 2000).

Conclusion

Unwork the Network

My theorization of tainted goods in this book is formed in critical dialogue with other notions of assemblage that have been conceived squarely within the contexts of marketing and actor-network theory. Particularly popular lately are marketing philosophies which posit people as increasingly irrelevant: while an individual human being may still be the "lead actor on the stage of consumption," so-called hybrid assemblage networks are redefining what constitutes an actor and an action within cultural and economic milieus.[1] Researchers strive to seek out potential "actants" (things that alter relations in assemblages) and the process of "actor-making" as it unfolds in practice. The technologies of self-tracking and self-making online allow for the assemblage of a new self: a digital doppelganger that is meant to seem solely the product of a person. The digital self evolves from the ongoing production of visual and textual content that offers evidence of development, progress, and betterment. More and more, there are assemblage-based attempts to weave together networks of products, services, or brands—as "heterogeneous allies"—in order to test the effectiveness of a particular market offering. The ultimate goal is integrated marketing communication and augmented product strategies, along with branding that incorporates non-human elements and social orders. Each order has its own "taste regimes and consumption patterns" that are always emerging and evolving, as it contains components that operate in the service of algorithmic interests, and that travel "under the representational radar."[2] And yet human actors persist in their (mis)perception of what constitutes a "good" product for them—envisioning brands, genres, fashions, values, and cultures as "real entities or social facts in relation to which they may act" upon a stage of self-fulfillment.[3]

Online networks of sharing and inclusion—fueled, in part, by consumerist ideologies of self-fulfillment—depend, of course, upon the exercise of exclusion of those who do not (or cannot) participate or perform the process of identity re-creation. As non- or pseudo-participants, they may be regarded as incomplete selves. In this book, I have argued that the assemblages made by Harrison, Genzken, Farmer, and Magor represent products and characters which fail to cohere and which possess a value that is indeterminate and in flux. Their works—while engaged with consumer objects, incorporating, complicating, and containing them in myriad ways—are disjunctive and dysfunctional to the extent that they cannot be networked, in any efficient sense. They bear (and sometimes suffer) a problematic, and at times pathetic, relationship to consumer and technological trends. Indeed, the best of such assemblages—which stage an awkward compositional dialogue with items of questionable currency—are prone to readings that allow for rumination on the predominating power of newness and novelty and the integral roles that these qualities play when it comes to orchestrating and marketing cultural experiences. Assemblage may still be conceived as a peripheral activity, one practiced by a relative few, developing an appetite for stuff that is, for the vast majority of us, undesirable and utterly irrelevant. I wish to dwell on the specific ways in which this found material is treated, with a host of gestures, ranging from care to contempt, anointment to insult, reverence to repeated abuse.

In *Tainted Goods*, I have argued that the assemblage phenomenon of dysfunctional consumption and problematic products is informed by historical, modernist, and theatrical traditions which combine literal content with absurdist, abstract, and existential elements. Another example of a historical source—one that seems particularly resonant these days—is Bertolt Brecht's play *Fear and Misery of the Third Reich* (which debuted in Paris on May 21, 1938): it portrays the Nazi regime as besieging its subjects with a mix of media ranging from the telephone to the radio to the newspaper, on display in every scene, so that the informational language of the regime infuses every aspect of domestic and public life. In one portion of the play, a "Jewish wife" rehearses and practices parting words to her non-Jewish husband: the language alternates between rage, melancholy, utter despair, absurdity, and sympathetic understanding. Delivered in fits and starts, the monologue is broken off and resumed several times, fragmenting the scene into many parts, but a variety of physical props remain, like the telephone.[4] The performance reveals anything but a unified self, reflecting a state of psychic disintegration. Indeed, the character exudes a palpable sense of disjunction. This is partly because of the manner in which her actions and words are actually reenacted: "her" words are quotations, reproductions of speeches that had been uttered by various others before, which Brecht had collected. While Walter Benjamin described this phenomenon as "quotability" (*Zitierbarkeit*), Brecht used the term "gestic dramaturgy," in which actors must "be able to space (*sperren*) [their] gestures the way that the typesetter spaces type." Benjamin observed that the "discovery and construction of gesus is nothing other than a retranslation of the methods of montage—so crucial to radio and film—from a technological process back into a human one."[5] Such figures on stage are not convincingly coherent characters, and yet they are striving to somehow *keep it together*, despite their predicament. They are compromised by the strategies of quotation, and perceived by the audience as mediatized beings that have been subjugated rather than fulfilled, with bodies burdened by the humiliating ordeal of incorporating information and technology. The role of abstraction in Brecht's plays, expressed in forms that frustrate informational exchange, is comparable to the pseudo-figures expressed in *tainted goods* assemblages. Brecht devised fundamental diagrams of theatrical encounter called *Grundmodelle*, or primary models, in which the social relations depicted do not "belong" to any single character, but are instead rendered through the features of the surrounding space. Accordingly, the emphasis was put on stage design that made it possible to represent abstract social schemes graphically—and offered the stage set as a dynamic system that (dys)functions in dialogue with its human contents. Brecht's sets were often meant to unframe the figure on stage, dissolving the "characters" into the support structures surrounding them, and redistributing dramatic agency across a number of bodies, both organic and inorganic. Gestic dramaturgy freed the events depicted on stage from attribution to any particular individual, replacing the ontology of character with an abstract diagram or "network" of action.

Face (Sculptural) Facts: Formats are Foul

Partly because of its structural relationship to such historical (and modernist) sources, *tainted goods* works may, indeed, be read as enacting a dysfunctional dialogue with the notion of the network subject. In the case of the assemblages treated in this book, this dialogue is performed in terms of tense exchanges between human-scaled, sculptural materiality and the online world. In his recent book *After Art*, David Joselit explores what happens when digital reproduction and media technologies take hold of art, causing the unit of aesthetic analysis to shift from individual works to virtually unlimited masses of images. Joselit recalls Benjamin's association of aura with site specificity: while a work belongs to a certain time and place, it can possess the authority of a witness. Reproduction, particularly within online environments, serves to unhinge a work from its site, making it more nomadic; it can change format, and experience "cascading chains of relocation and remediation." Instead of the "radiating nimbus of authenticity and authority underwritten by site specificity, we have the value of saturation, of being everywhere at once. In place of aura, there is buzz."[6] Referring to assemblages by Harrison, Joselit discusses how artists may manipulate the situational nature of content. This manipulation depends, in part, on the notion of *format* as a heterogeneous and provisional structure which channels content. In contrast to artistic mediums, such as painting and video—which are relatively limited and limiting because they call forth singular objects and limited visual practices—formats regulate image currencies or "aggregate content" by modulating their force, speed, and clarity; they can store such currency like a battery, stage extravagant expenditures, or "furnish fantastic landscapes for prosaic commodities to develop new behaviors—new social lives …"[7] What matters is not the production of new content but its *retrieval* in intelligible patterns through acts of reframing, capturing, reiterating, and documenting. "What counts, in other words, is how widely and easily images connect: not only to messages, but to other social currencies like capital, real estate, politics, and so on. In economies of image overproduction connectivity is key." For Joselit, art now exists as a fold, a disruption, or an event within a production of images.[8] Value is derived from searchability—its susceptibility to being found, recognized, or profiled. Accordingly, the goal of (art) institutions is to reach a certain level of saturation, or widespread connectivity, beyond which an image can function as a brand. Cookies or identity tags are essential in the globalized art world, in which success requires a quantum of identity signifiers (e.g., eBay mining) that may be easily communicated when referring to any particular work.[9] Artworks "must develop ways to build networks into their form by, for example, *reframing*, *capturing*, *reiterating*, and *documenting* existing content—all aesthetic procedures that explicitly presume a network as their 'ground'." This presumption must rely completely on content that is *seamlessly* compatible with easily digestible narrative structures that take shape within contexts operating separately from the exhibition venue. Divorced from the material matter of the sculptural experience, these structures result in branding effects that are said to matter in the marketing sense—a saturating impact that may be associated with a community-building ethos and progressive values. As the marketing theorist Celeste Condit argues, such values may be identified with social capital, and should allow for a social media experience that facilitates the format, and an audience's participatory perception of shared beliefs and symbol-sharing.[10] The format phenomenon is tied to a proliferation of exhibition footage and verbal commentary online. This discourse is supposedly "tested" by a variety of users with competing views, but ultimately fashioned into a story with characters, a history, and a singular conceptual direction—resulting in narrative that seems forged from deliberation and mutual understanding, one that signifies a "symbolic sharing of community" that is fully mediated.[11]

Joselit helpfully suggests that the power of assemblages by artists such as Harrison "lies in its staging of a performative mode of looking through which the single image and the network are visible *at once.*"[12] In a limited sense, I would agree that these works allow semantic space for an interpretation that addresses and potentially critiques—rather than uncritically mimics or follows—shifts from an object-based to a network aesthetics premised on the emergence of form from populations of images. This emergence is a phenomenon that unfolds in time, and may be narrated. In the case of tainted goods, it is essential, in my view, to offer a narrative that is primarily (but not exclusively) rooted in a first-hand, materialist engagement with sculptural displays within the gallery space. With its presentation of ready-made content and characters, the format phenomenon should never be permitted to fully infiltrate and distract from the potential of that on-site, bodily and performative engagement to provoke unruly insights and unforeseen reactions. Such reactions can conflict with formatted content, and may occur while circulating about the work itself—potentially with other viewers, with whom one may discuss and debate what or who the work may be about. It is this experience—of course inevitably formed with some awareness of online marketing messages—that results in a unique narrative that retains qualities that are untested, arguably unconvincing, and perhaps untrue. In this regard, then, I would accept the constraints of the "traditional" and auratic interpretive method, directed inward to the object as their organizing principle. Needless to say, by doing so, my method reifies the art object, and yet, as I have tried to demonstrate, tainted goods operate in ways that problematize and complicate this organizing process.

Muster the Marginal (or a Moment), Deal with (Some) Doubt, Relish (a Bit of) Redundancy

I have tried to argue that the onus is, in part, on the beholder of tainted goods to recognize the *possible* importance—rather than the undisputed value of format—of entertaining and maintaining a condition of challenging contemplation while confronting exhibitions featuring these works. I choose to make a go at striving to deal with doubts about what is being depicted, and how such displays might supply a commentary on the struggling state of selfhood in our time. Such imagery of the self may be debatable on multiple levels: conceptually, culturally, and compositionally. Viewers can and should argue about what is presented, and no single claim should ever attain the static status of certainty. Every reading—whether spoken in situ with witty aplomb or perhaps posted online with a sense of intuitive immediacy—should always be susceptible to critique or met with comments about its absurd or inaccurate qualities. Tainted goods cannot engage in certain forms of social commentary, such as satire, which traditionally is focused on specific targets, conceptually confined to a single individual or group. But broader and speculative kinds of critique are possible precisely because of (not despite) the disparate nature of these particular works, and their resistance to spoon-fed explanation. Relevant in this regard is Donald Judd's undefined definition of an aesthetic category for "specific objects." As Mary Leclère has discussed, Judd believed that something can only qualify as a category if it is sufficiently "inspecific" and unstable in identity, and hence open to dispute and debate.[13] This element of doubt and ambivalence contrasts with aesthetic sensibilities that comfortably supply a guarantee of conviction, that rise above the level of mere interest. As with Judd, central to my notion of the tainted goods category is the "obdurate identity" of sculptural material in itself, supplying an aspect that must operate in tension with the formation of a clear-cut subjectivity (belonging to the artist or anyone else). This ensures that the work is never fully resigned to its own reification, as a coherent character or consumable: it resists being a conventional "good" or commodity.

I am reminded of Georges Didi-Huberman's treatment of movie extras or *figurants*, "… a banal word, a word for the 'man without qualities' of a setting, of an industry, of a spectacular management of 'human resources'; but, also, it is an unfathomable word, a word from the labyrinths that every figure conceals." Within the economy of cinematography, extras are "an accessory of humanity which serves as a framework for the role of the central heroes, the real actors in the story, the protagonists, as they are called."[14] They are not merely part of the set. They are undoubtedly human, despite their seeming silence and their usual lack of agency within the central story. But they are *arguably* both actors and non-actors; for viewers, they tend to exist in the plural only. As such they may more easily be labeled as an Other. Normally, they are missing the individuation that makes up the "passionate complexity of the character, of the actor, or the subject of the action."[15] As with movie extras, tainted goods characters are of course beheld by viewers conditioned to compare them with more protagonistic personages— those playing leading roles, as it were. Existing, and persisting, on the margins, they do exhibit features with which audiences may identify, albeit tentatively. The viewer needs to project, in order to *construct* them as individuals, always acknowledging this imaginative leap as dysfunctionally running counter to conventional forms of consumption, potentially taking on tragic and comic qualities. In this regard, Agnes Heller has theorized "tragicomedies" which stage existential characters that cannot play roles with an easily personified historical importance. And any conflicts or incidents that occur are stylized to the degree that they are able to represent a notion of selfhood amounting to "not generalization or idealization, but the presentation of significant marginality as the carrier of the human condition ..." Crucial to this notion is that the (theatrical) display allows for individuals (both performers and beholders) to accept forms of absurdity as an integral component of playing the role of occupying the peripheries of a (networked) world in which conforming and confining conditions pervade and predominate, at all times.[16]

As I have discussed, these assemblages perform in this way partly because of their juxtaposition of literal, found things with abstract shapes that seem studio-crafted. Incorporating makeshift material, they tend to refer to several display contexts simultaneously, often in abrupt and unresolved ways. And yet when confronting such complicated compositions, one is weighed down by a doubt that lingers and sometimes pesters, a condition that is linked to the possible presence of redundancy. This condition is identified with a sense of the repetitious and the (merely) recycled. All of the artists treated in this book consistently include imagery and objects that seem "crafted" and the consequence of compositional care. And yet they make a point of re-introducing and re-inserting particular shapes, while maintaining a measured sense of variation and difference—in terms of how these objects are (re) displayed, (re)staged, and (re)situated. Remaining within a predominantly sculptural mode, they never fall prey to practices of postmodern pastiche, a value-neutral mashing together of styles which, like kitsch, thrives on cultural technologies of rapid reproducibility. Tainted goods promote speculation about whether the work has actually resisted the neutralizing effect of repetition. From without, repetition is practiced by cultural agencies of appropriation, duplication, and veneration. From within, there is a danger of self-repetition as well, requiring preventive measures against signification of nameable styles and signature products. Indeed, Beckett's strategy was to misremember earlier efforts in his successive works, recollecting while always distorting. Declining "naked" versions of repetition, Beckett practiced a "clothed" approach, which "puts difference on display; it is repetition that signals the impossibility of repetition—that, even as it indicates what is repeated, it insures its absolute indeterminacy."[17] In the first and second acts of *Happy Days*, for instance, Winnie offers a clothed repetition of dialogue which Beckett had previously employed. In 1961, Beckett composed Winnie's lines while thinking of *Waiting for Godot*'s popularity, a work in which nothing happens, twice (Godot never appears). In *Happy Days*, something does happen, twice (Winnie appears), which operates in tension with our dramatic expectations, sustaining our condition of unknowing and avoiding the threat of familiarity and habit. Hence, the development of a Beckett *oeuvre* became more problematic as a marketable concept. Rather, his work seemed more like a dialogue between coherence and unravelment; his practice questioned the idea of a progressive evolution, one that follows the moral imperative of striving to move forward. Crucially, the trope of failure (to go on, to advance) still continues to operate, instilling a sense of comic irrelevance and irony that, quite reliably, will rub some audiences the wrong way.

Some critics have been quite dismissive of the ability of assemblages to serve as vehicles for critical contemplation. This attitude is partly rooted in the recognition of unmonumental and DIY tendencies in contemporary art as trends—and as an established style, which needless to say, may be subject to marketing apparatuses and assigned associated market values. I have tried to demonstrate that the structural qualities of tainted goods do have a potential to be displayed and interpreted in ways that make such popularity less central. For one thing, they should encourage a comparative and evaluative awareness of works that are challenging and those that are not (or that resist rising above the level of trend). This critical awareness does not depend upon knowledge of contexts pertaining to particular artists or their respective scenes and milieus, content that may be seductively summarized and encapsulated endlessly on the fair and biennial circuit. Rather, it reflects a belief (or faith) in the aesthetic potential of a *focused encounter* with a series of assemblage works within a specific exhibition venue. And I must stress that this awareness must always remain a potential, never a guarantee. After all, assemblages have just as much potential to be absorbed into the experience economy as any other kind of practice. The beholder should grapple with doubts—about the ability of the work itself to signify and supply insight, and about his or her ability to speculate in a satisfactory way about these tainted subjects and objects. They should never stop being dysfunctional and disjunctive.

As Juliane Rebentisch has argued, "interested art" should not be read as disavowing itself as art, becoming a mere means for the efficient transmission of identity-political or social issues. Aesthetic form is always in process, in a state of becoming. Structurally speaking, this process may promise the beholder the possibility that it might effect changes in consciousness because it reflectively distances the familiar. Art should not apologize for being tied to a praxis that cannot be translated directly into action or immediately into cognition. Art that is worthwhile will undermine simple identification with the work, instead compelling me to have a performative and self-reflective relation to the object that must subjectively deal with my own silent baggage of cultural and social assumptions. Hence, the meanings that come to appear in the work are never truly warranted by the work—and so the viewer has to reflect on his or her own productivity in the creation of relations of meaning.[18]

It is important to strive for a dialogue with those seeking to situate such discourse within the realm of contemporary exhibitions, devoted to displays that may signify the present and the past, the new and the obsolete. To qualify as tainted goods, works must combine items from divergent temporal (and display) contexts that convey a spirit of refusal—a snub to relentless expectations for branded and seamless experiences that seem novel and provide immediate enjoyment. While there are scholars that address these phenomena in profound and earnest ways, dealing with works that are historically remote—such as Didi-Huberman—I wish to do so in a manner that makes room for the marginal and the ridiculous.[19] Amelia Groom, for instance, has made the case that we should step away from the worn paradigms of (artistic) ego, and conceive of time from the perspective of the artwork itself, against the notion of art production as a conscious, heroic, step-by-step execution from an idea to a predetermined end. Groom wants to draw attention to how exhibitions may do away with consensually agreed-upon chronology and the confines of museological categories, assuming

> that the time and place in which a thing was made should not shut it off from other times and places. Works of art can bear witness to the context of their conception and fabrication, but to treat them as pedagogical historic documents is to suffocate them.[20]

But it is a sense of disjunction that is crucial to achieving a contemporary enactment of beholding that is inclusive of unconventional conceptions of time which may be mocked by conservative critics—as paradoxical and ridiculous—in the name of scholarly objectivity. For Giorgio Agamben, those that truly belong to their time are those who "neither perfectly coincide with it nor adjust themselves to its demands. They are thus in this sense irrelevant." Tainted goods provide me with the *material means* to perceive the obscurity of the present, as it is only through my untimeliness that I am equipped to grasp my time, my age. Within a sculptural setting, it is crucial to court a relationship with the present that "adheres to it through a disjunction." This is a now that refuses its nowness, indebted to Benjamin's concept of "now time" (*Jetztzeit*), which is not oriented to a projected, indefinitely deferred savior (a heroic force) but rather the notion of revolution as an ongoing latent presence. Agamben argues that the key to being relevant is a sense of disconnection and out-of-jointness:

> That which impedes access to the present is precisely the mass of what for some reason (its traumatic character, its excessive nearness)

we have not managed to live. The attention to this "unlived" is the life of the contemporary. And to be contemporary means in this sense to return to a present where we have never been.[21]

Notes

1 For an excellent, summarizing guide to such issues from the marketer's standpoint, see Robin Canniford and Domen Bajde's Introduction to Canniford and Bajde, eds., *Assembling Consumption: Researching Actors, Networks, and Markets* (New York: Routledge, 2016), esp. 8.

2 See, for instance, A. Joy and J. F. Sherry, "Speaking of Art as Embodied Imagination: A Multisensory Approach to Understanding Aesthetic Experience," *Journal of Consumer Research* 30, no. 2 (2003): 259–82.

3 See Robert V. Kozinets and John F. Sherry, Jr., "The Autothemataludicization Challenge: Spiritualizing Consumer Culture through Playful Communal Co-Creation," in Diego Rinallo, Linda Scott, and Pauline Maclaran, eds., *Consumption and Spirituality* (New York: Routledge, 2013), 242–66. See also Fuat A. Firat and Nikolesh Dholakia, *Consuming People: From Political Economy to Theaters of Consumption* (London: Routledge, 1998).

4 For helpful treatment of Brecht's play and its significance, see Devin Fore, *Realism after Modernism: The Rehumanization of Art and Literature* (Cambridge, MA: MIT Press, 2012), 139–40, 175.

5 See Michael W. Jennings, ed., *Walter Benjamin: Selected Writings* (Cambridge, MA: Harvard University Press, 2005), vol. 2, 584.

6 Joselit, *After Art* (Princeton: Princeton University Press, 2013), 14, 16.

7 Ibid., 55.

8 Ibid., 56, 89.

9 In this regard, Joselit is one of the very few to provide detailed discussion of the influential marketing research of B. Joseph Pine II and James H. Gilmore in relation to art practice: a "good" is a customized commodity, a "service" is a customized good, an "experience" is a customized service, and a "transformation" is a customized service that promises authenticity, in which art facilitates a "special kind of currency exchange where cultural difference is assessed and traded like yen, renminbi, euros, and dollars" (84). For further comments, see my Introduction.

10 See Condit, "The Functions of Epideictic," *Communication Quarterly* 33 (1985): 284–99. See also Lawrence Rosenfeld, "The Practical Celebration of Epideictic," in Eugene E. White, ed., *Rhetoric in Transition: Studies in the Nature and Uses of Rhetoric* (University Park: Pennsylvania University Press, 1980) and Dale Sullivan, "The Ethos of the Epideictic Encounter," *Philosophy and Rhetoric* 26, no. 2 (1993): 113–33.

11 Indeed, some psychological research into screen-based marketing phenomena has focused on brand associations and their connections to mental representations that individual viewers hold of themselves, drawing parallels with TV and social-media formats. Each consumer may identify with certain characters with relative ease, making use of a branded narrative to construct and cultivate a particular conception of the self, engaging in projection and

"narrative processing," signaled by the presence of a structure that provides temporal and relational organization and a basis for casual inferencing. For helpful commentary on screen-based communal aspects of consumerism, see Cristel A. Russell, Andrew T. Norman, and Susan E. Heckler, "People and 'Their' Television Shows: An Overview of Television Connectedness," in L. J. Shrum, ed., *The Psychology of Entertainment Media: Blurring the Lines Between Entertainment and Persuasion* (New Jersey and London: Lawrence Erlbaum Associates, 2004) 275–89.

12 Joselit, *After Art*, 39, 45, 95–96. Joselit makes the case that artists need to recognize and exploit the realms of the format and the network in newly creative and progressive ways and that interpreters need to develop critical models which no longer prioritize auratic objects—in order to contend competently with the phenomenon of image circulation, presumably pertaining to what is now widely considered to be high-value (i.e., densely circulating) art.

13 For helpful discussion of these issues, see Leclère, "From Specific Objects to Specific Subjects: Is there (still) Interest in Pluralism?" *Afterall: A Journal of Art, Context and Enquiry* 11 (Spring–Summer 2005): 9–16. See also Judd, "Specific Objects" (1965) and "Local History" (1964), in Judd, *Complete Writings 1959–1975* (1975) (Halifax and New York: Nova Scotia College of Art and Design and New York University Press, 2005), esp. 184 and 151.

14 See Didi-Huberman, "People Exposed: People as Extras," in Eric Alliez and Peter Osborne, eds., *Spheres of Action: Art and Politics* (London and Cambridge, MA: Tate Publishing and MIT Press, 2013), 33–44, esp. 38–39.

15 Ibid., 39.

16 In Kafka's *The Metamorphosis*, Gregor Samsa is not surprised to learn that he has been transformed into an insect. A key feature of Kafka's story is that there is no curse: Gregor's previous life, with his family, was itself absurd. The plot makes an everyday destiny appear in an existential light. One becomes what one is. Gregor was treated like an insect, he accepted it, and so he became an insect. And his family, like the reader, end up accepting him as a bug. This storyline reflects the central conceit of complying with the absurd as if it were natural, but only as a result of a struggle with preconceptions about what constitutes a fully-fledged character or protagonist. See Heller, *Immortal Comedy: The Comic Phenomenon in Art, Literature, and Life* (Oxford: Lexington Books, 2005), 94–124.

17 For relevant comments, see H. Porter Abbott, "Late Modernism: Samuel Beckett and the Art of the Oeuvre," in Enoch Brater and Ruby Cohn, eds., *Around the Absurd: Essays on Modern and Postmodern Drama* (Ann Arbor: University of Michigan Press, 1990), 75. To discuss clothed repetition, Deleuze variously employs the terms "vetu," "masqué," "déguisé," and "trevesti," as opposed to "nu" (naked). See Deleuze, *Différence et repetition* (Paris: Presses Universitaires de France, 1968), 36–39.

18 See Rebentisch, *Aesthetics of Installation Art* (2003), trans. D. Hendrickson with G. Jackson (Berlin: Sternberg Press, 2012), 271. The works in a sense are "looking back" and offer meanings that I have not intentionally made or objectively discovered in the object. These unexpected meanings happen

when I give myself over to the "substance" of the concrete as a means for reflection that is reducible neither to theoretical nor practical reason—and that is not sublated by modernist objectivism which uses the work as an instrument for disinterested contemplation.

19 In this regard, I would refer to Mieke Bal's now-classic formulation of "preposterous" (literally "pre" + "post") history, in which she treats a diverse array of artistic "quotations" of Caravaggio as an ongoing conversation between pasts, presents, and futures. See Bal, *Quoting Caravaggio: Contemporary Art, Preposterous History* (Chicago: University of Chicago Press, 1999).

20 Groom's edited volume is meant, in part, to help facilitate this goal. See her thoughtful introduction to *Time* (London and Cambridge, MA: Whitechapel and MIT Press, 2013), 12–25. The book emphasizes tendencies to embrace outdated technologies and outmoded materials, restaging downtrodden possibilities, sometimes repeatedly. Groom stresses that such displays and compositions should avoid a winking pastiche of appropriated styles and a nostalgic immersion in a fixed, absent past.

21 See Agamben, "What is Contemporary?" (2008) in Agamben, *What is an Apparatus?* (Stanford: Stanford University Press, 2009), 39–56, 39. The "unlived" for me tends, always in a partial sense, toward phenomena that resist being packaged and cannot be spoon-fed.

Index

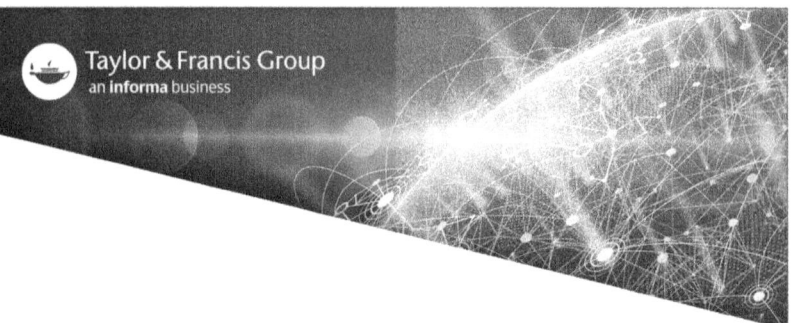
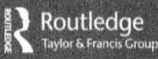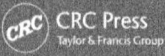

For Product Safety Concerns and Information please contact our EU
representative GPSR@taylorandfrancis.com
Taylor & Francis Verlag GmbH, Kaufingerstraße 24, 80331 München, Germany